CHILDREN: HANDLE WITH CARE

A critical analysis of the development of
Intermediate Treatment

John Paley
&
David Thorpe

August 1974

Published by National Youth Bureau,
37 Belvoir Street, Leicester LE1 6SL

Price £2.00 (inc. postage)

SBN 90209574 9

The National Youth Bureau is an independent Charitable Trust, and is the national centre for information, research and training services in the social education of young people in England and Wales.

CONTENTS

	Preface	1
1	Intermediate Treatment and Delinquency	3
2	The Regional Schemes	14
3	Ten Projects: Description	27
4	Ten Projects: Analysis	52
5	Finding Delinquents	74
6	A Continuum of Care	84
7	Beginning Intermediate Treatment	94
	Appendix	105
	Notes	107

PREFACE

This book began as a piece of work commissioned by a group of people working in intermediate treatment projects in various parts of the country, who met together for the first time in October 1973. Some of the projects with which they were associated had been set up by local authorities invited by the Department of Health and Social Security to participate in its own "Intermediate Treatment Project" (a report of which appeared last November); all of them were exploring the possibilities of intermediate treatment legislation in the context of their own work. It emerged that they shared a concern about the way in which the concept was being developed at regional and local level, and that they felt the need to make available an account of their own experience which might serve as a supplement, or alternative, to regional planning and the D.H.S.S. publications. The group has since become known as the Intermediate Treatment Development Group.

At first, the book was conceived purely as a description and analysis of the projects. Although a study of this kind remains at the heart of the present work, it was inevitable that the book should grow in concept as it was being written, and that the authors should go beyond the original brief as their own ideas and attitudes developed. It was also inevitable, perhaps, that not all the members of the Development Group would approve of the direction in which the book moved as a result. In the event, most of them have continued to support it, while making various criticisms, and have supplied material which is incorporated into Chapter 3. The one exception is Dallington Lodge. This project has informed us that, because of the general structure of the book, they feel unable to associate themselves with it. However, as we feel that the work of this project is important, references to it have been kept in, and a description of it, based on reports generally available, has been included along with the others. At the same time, the opinions expressed in this book are entirely the authors' own: the members of the Intermediate Treatment Development Group are not committed to the views presented in any part of it although, with this one exception, they have all given their support to its publication.

The book falls roughly into three sections. The first two chapters retrace the steps of the Home Office White Paper, *Children in Trouble,* and of the two D.H.S.S. publications, and offer criticism of regional planning. Chapters 3 and 4 discuss in detail the work of the ten projects that make up the Development Group and begin an analysis of the techniques and approaches which they employ. Chapters 5, 6 and 7 are more developmental in intention, drawing out from the analysis of the projects, and the theoretical and critical material of the first two chapters, a "theory" of intermediate treatment as a "continuum of care". We have tried, in this final section, to formulate an account of the social and political context in which intermediate treatment will take place, of the resources and planning it may require, and of the theoretical and administrative framework in terms of which it can be conceived. Though it would be impossible to separate out the ideas and contributions of each author in detail, it can be said that while the first two sections owe most to John Paley, the third is primarily the work of David Thorpe.

So many people have influenced and encouraged the writing of the book that it would be impossible to name them all. A list of those associated with the projects on whose experience so much of it is based, and which supplied us with some of the descriptions in Chapter 3, will be found in Appendix A. Our thanks go to them for their contributions, and for their help, ideas and support. In addition we should like to thank the following for comments and criticisms: Chris Andrews, Mike Bacon, Ken Exton, Richard Harthill, Christine Matthews, Judy Miller, Terry Powley, Brian Stimpson and John Ewen, Director of the National Youth Bureau, through whose good offices the book appears as an NYB publication.

1 INTERMEDIATE TREATMENT AND DELINQUENCY

The past 150 years have seen a gradual change of policy in our society with regard to the ways in which young offenders are punished and treated. The most important of these changes have occurred since 1945, with the legislation of 1948, 1963 and 1969 increasingly emphasising the aim of preventing delinquency rather than punishing it. The 1963 Children and Young Persons Act enabled local authorities to finance provision for young people who were at risk of being committed or received into care. The 1969 C.Y.P.A. goes even further in that it obliges local authorities to set up schemes, on a regional basis, for the treatment of young offenders (or potential offenders) within the community, and empowers the juvenile courts to require such treatment in the case of a court appearance.

This evolving policy of treatment within the community has parallels in recent legislation providing for the mentally ill and handicapped (1959 Mental Health Act), adult criminals (1972 Criminal Justice Act) and the physically incapacitated (1970 Chronically Sick and Disabled Act). These acts are all designed to provide and expand a range of social services within the community for those who would otherwise, because of dangers and difficulties to themselves and/or society, be placed in institutions.

This, then, is the starting point for an analysis of intermediate treatment: the provision of a range of services within the community for those at risk of becoming, or those who have already become, "delinquent". We propose to begin with those delinquent young people. We shall ask: "Who are they, and why do they come before the courts?" — for if we can answer this question, we may be able to develop a concept of treatment which is in some measure a response to their needs and experience.

Delinquency

Children in Trouble, the white paper which first made official mention of intermediate treatment[1], begins with some general remarks on juvenile deliquency. We shall do the same. We would like to discuss three broad aspects of the phenomenon known as "deliquency", and it is our intention to develop an account of intermediate treatment which will take into consideration some of the points mentioned under the following headings:

a) The causes of delinquency
b) The experience of delinquency
c) The identification of delinquency

By "causes" of delinquency, we mean such factors as the social and economic circumstances in which a child grows up, the environment from which he comes, his family background, his education. Psychological difficulties and abnormalities can also be placed under this heading. By the "experience" of delinquency we mean the patterns of relationship, attitude and behaviour of which delinquency consists, and the forms of association (or non-association), and the kinds of norm that tend to foster it. Finally, by the "identification" of delinquency, we mean the processes whereby delinquency is defined by the community, and whereby the delinquent himself is picked out – by police, parents, youth and social workers, or teachers. Under this heading, it is also convenient to include the processes of law themselves. We shall consider each of these aspects in turn and discuss the implications for treatment.

The Causes of Delinquency

This is the factor which seems to have received most emphasis in official literature. For example, *Children in Trouble* states, of delinquent behaviour:

> "Frequently such behaviour is no more than an incident in the pattern of a child's normal development. But sometimes it is a response to unsatisfactory family or social circumstances, a result of boredom in and out of school, an indication of maladjustment or immaturity, or a symptom of a deviant, damaged or abnormal personality."[2]

This is not something we wish to question, although we do feel it is possible to overstress the psychological abnormality of delinquents. But what are the implications for treatment? Leaving aside, for the time being, abnormal psychology, it would seem that if we are to take deprivation seriously we should be trying to ameliorate the circumstances in which the delinquent child or young person finds himself. If the delinquent tends to come from a a certain kind of deprived environment or background, we should, within the framework of the act, be trying to overcome these disadvantages – to bring him into contact with a healthier environment and provide him with the opportunity for activities, interests and relationships that he has hitherto been unable to enjoy. This is, in fact, the kind of emphasis that we find in the official publications:

> "The aim will be to bring the young person into contact with a new environment, and to secure his participation in some constructive activity."[3]

> "The object of the treatment will be to bring the child into contact with a different environment and to give him the opportunity of forming new personal relationships and developing new interests . . . The purpose of the court . . . will have been to use the opportunity presented by intermediate treatment to enrich the child's environment and

assist his development. The treatment available should therefore provide a means for broadening his experience in ways likely to be beneficial to his development as an individual and as a member of society."[4]

We should note that there are two considerations here. Firstly, and perhaps more relevantly to the concept of "treatment", in providing the young person with such opportunities we are trying to overcome factors that give rise to delinquency. It is a simple matter of cause and effect. We dislike, or disapprove of, certain patterns of behaviour and seek to eliminate some of the factors that give rise to them. At least, we try to lessen the importance of these factors, or introduce new factors which will have the opposite effect. Secondly, however, there is a consideration of a more normal character: there are disadvantaged children who could do with a break, who deserve opportunities they have so far been denied.

Two further comments should, perhaps, be made. A programme such as intermediate treatment, which is designed for particular children manifesting symptoms of deprivation, does not make such sense independently of a wider programme – that of a general attack on the social, economic and educational problems of deprivation.

We are open to a charge of dishonesty if we attend to the problem only where it breaks out in the form of undesirable behaviour instead of attempting to combat it at source. The disadvantaged young people who could do with a break are not just those who appear in court. *Children in Trouble* makes a similar point when it talks of treatment not being restricted to groups of delinquents alone,[5] although this condition emerges in D.H.S.S. publications with a somewhat different emphasis – that treatment in the company of others is part of the therapy.[6]

Moreover, "new environment" ought to mean what it says, if taken seriously. One can be forgiven for wondering how far it is true of the majority of facilities now appearing in the regional schemes, especially if the most convenient facility is to be used in any given case, as has been stated in some areas. We are not suggesting that the (literally) hundreds of youth clubs and scout troops that are listed in the schemes have, after all, no part to play in intermediate treatment; but it is doubtful whether, in many cases, they can really provide "contact with a new environment".

However, despite these reservations, we shall restrict our attention to what can realistically be achieved within the framework of the Act. This is to accept that social and youth work attention will inevitably be focused on young people who do manifest the "symptoms" of deprivation more energetically than their fellows (for whatever reasons), and that the resources which will be available for intermediate treatment will necessarily be limited by financial and political considerations.

The Experience of Delinquency

The features of delinquency discussed in the previous section tend to focus attention on the individual child, or the individual action, and relate it to its background and environment. Now, however, we wish to draw attention away from the concrete, from a particular child or action, and towards the situation of a young person within a group of his fellows, and the context of an action within the system of attitudes, norms and relationships which support it. There are two aspects to this:

i) It is possible to see the individual as part of a group or "culture", and to understand his actions in the context of the norms and attitudes operating within that culture. To this extent, we can think of the group itself, and its framework of norms and attitudes, as logically prior to the individual members. Just as our own actions are, to a great extent, determined by the social norms of the groups to which we belong, so the actions of delinquents can be conceived as determined by delinquent norms.

ii) While this is to adopt a slightly different perspective on delinquency, it is not to reject what has been said about its causes. Within this perspective, the various causal factors may be thought of, not as bringing about individual actions, but as giving rise to a structure of norms and attitudes in the context of which delinquent behaviour takes place. This structure, operating within a group or culture, is the medium through which the deprivations of background and environment connect with delinquent action.

What is the basis, then, for this structure of delinquent norms? Ultimately, it is a matter of achievement and self-esteem. Given our acceptance of the environmental causes of delinquency, this should not be surprising. Coming from deprived and disadvantaged backgrounds, these young people tend not to be successful in society's terms, and at the tasks with which society provides them. The effect is to create what has been called "failed identity", a self-concept which includes marked elements of inadequacy, worthlessness and vulnerability. Such an identity is, in itself, unaccpetable to any human being, and it is therefore necessary to find alternative criteria for achievement and success. For some young people, delinquency provides just such criteria. Either by forming associations with others like themselves, or by rejecting associations altogether, they find a basis for status and self-esteem by committing anti-social acts. This is the central feature of delinquent association, perhaps, though there are others linked with it: for example, the way in which the group (or individual) reacts to external agencies, particularly those which are perceived as threatening in some way – police, schools, social workers. Often, their relations with these agencies are such as to reinforce, rather than weaken, the structure of norms and attitudes which constitutes their delinquency.

The fact that the delinquent's activity may be supported and reinforced by the form of his associations complicates matters. In the previous section, the provision of new opportunities for disadvantaged young people was represented as a simple matter of cause and effect: if we seek to combat delinquency, we must try either to eliminate some of the factors that give rise to it, or introduce new ones. But is it as simple as this? Can these new opportunities alone have a significant effect on patterns of behaviour that are already established? Such a pattern may become, to a great extent, independent of the factors that originally gave rise to it: for it may be supported by the continued association of the members of a delinquent peer-group (and reinforced by the group's relations with external agencies); or it may be maintained by an individual's continuing fear and rejection of associations of any kind. The point is that if delinquent attitudes can become detached, in this way, from the conditions that promoted them, young people who have developed certain responses to various factors in their environment may not find it easy to give them up even when some of these factors are eliminated. The effect of these factors on their behaviour "cannot, after all, be compared to the impact of one billiard ball upon another. The difference is that delinquent behaviour – like human behaviour in general – is learned, and that, once a pattern of behaviour has been formed in response to a particular situation, it will not necessarily disappear with a change in that situation".[7]

It is for this reason that the attack on deprivation, and the provision of new opportunities for disadvantaged young people, cannot be separated from a special kind of work with those who have established delinquent attitudes. This work will be an attempt not merely to provide the young people with new opportunities, contact with a new environment, and so on, but also to intervene in the processes which help to maintain delinquents in their anti-social attitudes.

What, then, are the implications for treatment under this heading? In a single word: group work. If the foregoing argument is correct, it appears that our resources should be focused on the delinquent group, its attitudes, norms and relationships. Techniques must be found for "group intervention" and "group learning" – an attempt to diminish the importance of delinquent norms and replace them with more acceptable ones. There should be opportunities for young people to experience success in other than delinquent terms, and to renew their confidence in handling larger non-delinquent group situations like schools and youth clubs. In the case of the isolated individual, confidence in any kind of group situation may have to be renewed. There should also be an attempt to overcome the delinquents' attitudes towards external agencies, such as social workers, teachers and police, and to help them develop better relationships with adults generally and these adults in particular. This latter task spans two headings: it is both the provision of opportunities for new relationships with adults, and the promotion of attitudes within the group which will combat its norm structure.

Natural Groups

It may be observed that group work of this kind might best take place with natural, as opposed to artificial, groups, although work with artificial groups is the basis for most of the projects represented in this book. This observation can be accepted: ideally, work with natural groups may be preferable. Two comments, however, can be made. Firstly, work with natural groups does not easily fit the legal framework, whereby individual children receive orders from the court. In a legal, and administrative, context, it is far more convenient to work with artificial groups. The natural group may be better handled on a detached basis, though whether such work qualifies as "intermediate treatment" is a question best left to semanticists and social services committees. There are, however, precedents. The National Childrens' Bureau Project, which works with young people in very much this kind of way, is called an intermediate treatment project.[8] This is, of course, entirely acceptable. We shall later argue that there is room for both approaches under the general rubric of intermediate treatment — the problem may be to persuade those who hold the purse strings. The second comment concerns the disadvantages, if such there are, of working with artifical groups. Perhaps these are not too great. The important thing is the system of norms and attitudes which operate between delinquent young people as a result of certain kinds of deprivation. If children from similar backgrounds, who are members of similar groups, are brought together to form a new, artifical, group, we may anticipate that, although there will be some differences, the new group's structure will closely resemble that of the original ones. Certainly, the problems they will encounter (and which the social workers will encounter) are likely to be much the same. At any rate, experience does suggest that useful work can be done with artificial groups on these terms.

The Identification of Delinquency

The visibility of delinquency is a function not merely of delinquent activity but also of the response to such activity on the part of the general public, at least as represented by the media and the "agents of social control". As *Children in Trouble* concedes:

> "It is probably a minority of children who grow up without ever misbehaving in ways which may be contrary to the law."[9]

However, there are ways in which the natural, but sensationalist, exaggerations of the media may inflate general concern and create an atmosphere in which pressures are created which serve only to sensitize perceptions of delinquent activity all the more. As a result, we may all become more inclined to seize on some piece of behaviour and label it "delinquent". We may also observe that it is possible that the "agents of social control", especially the police, by yielding to these pressures, themselves affect the level of delinquent activity. If, for example, police activity is fairly low-key and tolerant (within certain limits), delinquency rates may be lower than if a "get tough" policy is adopted, when conviction rates, court appearances and the general visibility of delinquency will all increase. Such policies may become part of a general interactive cycle in which pressures can affect policies, and policies in turn, through their effect on the visibility of delinquency, can increase pressures. The worrying possibility is, of course, that if *Children in Trouble* is right, and it is a minority of children who do not at some time or another contravene the law, then the activities of such agencies may grossly exaggerate delinquent behaviour in general.

There is another reason why this is worrying. It is possible that the delinquents' experience of the police and the courts may, far from deterring them, confirm them in their delinquency. We have already suggested that delinquent activity may be sustained through the medium of the peer-group, which affords its members the opportunity of achievement in terms other than those sanctioned by society. For this reason, and for historical ones – previous police involvement with a family or neighbourhood, for example – such a group, or an individual, may maintain a suspicious and distrustful attitude towards the visible agents of society – a society which has imposed upon them the tasks at which they have failed. Abrasive contact with the police and the courts may only serve to confirm these suspicions and reinforce distrustful attitudes. Views about police, courts, social workers and teachers which have been passed on to the group may be confirmed, and the delinquent may come to adopt them, now strengthened, as his own. There is more failure, more suspicion, more distrust – and delinquent activity is not submerged, but encouraged.

A similar argument applies to those institutions which await the delinquent beyond the courts, the detention centres, attendance centres and, ultimately, approved schools or community homes. The same argument – and another one, that excessive familiarity with these institutions will add to the delinquent career a certain skill at playing according to the rules as long as the delinquent is in contact with them. And this skill can only make him more immune to their intended effects. Approved school figures on reconviction rates tend to confirm this conclusion.[10] Since it can cost up to £3,500 per year, per child (in London), to keep a young person in an approved school, this is an expensive way to fail. If the foregoing argument is correct, it may also be an unnecessary way to fail. Successive contact with such institutions only aggravates the young person's delinquent situation. Thus he becomes locked not merely in a cycle of deprivation, but also in a cycle of aggravation.

Once more we come to ask about the implications for treatment in this discussion – except that "treatment", under this heading, does not seem to be such an appropriate word. Perhaps it could be a function of all those involved in intermediate treatment – though in a much wider context than that alone – to maintain a barrier, or buffer, between the delinquent, or "pre-delinquent", and over-sensitized activity on the part of police, courts and media. This might apply particularly to social workers (some of whom see themselves in this kind of role already), youth workers and, perhaps, teachers. Not unnaturally, however, those who are more closely identified with institutions which are objects of delinquent suspicion may find it correspondingly more difficult to fulfil this function. Intermediate treatment itself could provide just such a buffer, if intermediate treatment requirements are constantly sought as an alternative to residential care and detention centres. If intermediate treatment is to act as a buffer in this way, however, constant negotiation will be required, and workers may become involved in activity which will appear to other agencies as protection of the delinquent (a view which is quite prevalent already). More generally, the attempt to keep young people out of care can be argued on other grounds: the apparent failure of the institutions, and the expense involved in maintaining children in care anyway. Perhaps a proportion of delinquents do need special care, residential treatment; but this proportion may be smaller than popularly imagined and, if this is true, intermediate treatment may be a viable alternative, combined with programmes of day-care, truancy schemes, trade-training schemes and short-stay care. This topic will be further explored in the final chapter.

Understanding Delinquents

If intermediate treatment is to be a means of keeping children out of care, it may be necessary to question some other current beliefs about delinquency. For it can be argued that the attitudes and values of many residential and field social workers, teachers, police and psychologists towards persistent delinquents are strongly influenced by theories of abnormal psychology. The D.H.S.S. booklet, *Intermediate Treatment Project,* makes the following qualification:

> "To use a negative definition, Intermediate Treatment is not likely to be adequate for the child whose difficulties of personality are severe or deeply rooted, whose home and family problems are intractable, or who has specific mental or physical handicaps."[11]

This is, of course, something with which one can readily agree. But the reference to "difficulties of personality" raises the problem of the relation of delinquency to psychological abnormality and emotional disturbance, factors which often weigh heavily in the formulation of treatment policies and programmes. The problem which arises when terms such as "emotional disturbance" are introduced resides not so much in the statement that there *is* a group of young people for whom intermediate treatment may not be adequate, as in the *identification* of the group in question. For which children is residential care necessary, and according to what criteria are they to be identified? How large is the group of young people whose "difficulties of personality are severe or deep-rooted"?

In question here is the application of a group of expressions, often used in connection with delinquency as an explanation, or quasi-explanation, of the delinquent's behaviour. "Difficulties of personality", "psychological abnormality" and "emotional disturbance" are but examples. These expressions, which readily fit the popular medical model of deviance, with its vocabulary of sickness and treatment, may mean either a great deal or virtually nothing. If they mean a great deal, then they must be part of some psychological theory that gives them meaning. It is not intended here to raise the problem of how far social workers and others can assess young people in these terms; but the question must be asked: what criteria are *in fact* used? – whether in relation to particular theories or not. The evidence suggests a certain looseness of application. Even among psychologists there is a tendency to see emotional disturbance where there may be only mischief and naughtiness. It is unfortunately true that, all too often, the evidences of emotional disturbance lie in the very acts which bring the child to the notice of the police and courts in the first place. What we cannot understand, or do not want to understand, is not understandable. And so, simply because the young person commits an act of violence, or truants from school, or habitually steals, there is reason for believing him emotionally disturbed. For what sane and mature person ever acts violently, becomes dissatisfied with schooling, or finds the need to take what is someone else's?

It is not, of course, to be denied that such acts *may* constitute evidence of psychological abnormality; but if they do so only in connection with other facts about the child and in relation to theories of personality which explain and support these facts. We are suggesting, however, that in a great many cases these supporting facts are absent and the case for emotional disturbance thin indeed.

It is usual to assess and classify children committed to care before deciding on an appropriate residential placement. This assessment is carried out by a multi-disciplinary team, which, despite its sophisticatiom, is often unable to find a suitable institution. A psychologist with several years' experience of working in an approved school has recently said this about assessment:

> "The implication of the procedure is that the child is abnormal on admission. He then passes through a screening process which ensures that his 'abnormality' will be confirmed. . . what is important is the underlying attitude which assumes that careful assessment is essential because the children are abnormal . . . the ultimate effect on the child is to fulfil the expectations of the role thrust upon him".[12]

The situation is complicated, and made even more chaotic, by the fact that such judgements – concerning the severity of personality disorders – are subject to local and personal variations. What passes without undue notice in the city may be unusual enough to attract attention in a rural area. A magistrate on an urban bench may recommend supervision, or even conditional discharge, in a case which a rural colleague may regard as "care order material". Moreover, the availability of residential places varies from area to area, so that whether or not a young person ends up in care can depend simply on where he lives. And, as we have already suggested, the visibility of his problems may, in the first place, depend on social work caseloads and police activity.

It should not be denied that use of the medical model may reflect a liberal and tolerant frame of mind, may reflect a rationale for the rejection of more obviously punitive measures in favour of more humane treatment. Liberal or not, however, the model is connected with the development of institutions and procedures which may be unnecessary and, at worst, damaging. More relevantly, perhaps, for those who hold the purse strings, they are expensive: in 1970-1, the estimated total national net expenditure on approved schools alone was £11,773,122.[13]

What actually happens, then, to the child who appears in court — if, indeed, he does so — is, to some extent, randomised. That is to say, he is subject to variables more significant than either the offence or his individual needs, his background or his psychological state, considered in objective terms. What happens to him may not be a realistic indication of his level of delinquency, or the degree of his psychological abnormality.

Our position is as follows: the great majority of delinquent young people are not emotionally or psychologically disturbed; the proportion of children who definitely need residential care is relatively small, and the proportion for whom intermediate treatment, in one form or another, is appropriate correspondingly large. To the D.H.S.S. statement that intermediate treatment is "an addition to supervision in the home, which may make the process more effective and may therefore reduce the numbers of children and young people for whom removal from home seems the only solution at present",[14] we would therefore add "substantially" between "therefore" and "reduce". In our view, intermediate treatment is primarily a means of keeping young people out of care. This is to repeat, but the repetition may unfortunately be necessary.

Just as one can question the alleged psychological differences between those who receive residential treatment and those who do not, so one can also suggest that the differences between children who offend regularly and consequently appear in court and children who are considered to be merely "at risk" usually have little to do with psychological stability. The difference is simply what it appears to be: a matter of persistent, reported delinquent behaviour. Rather than any emotional disturbance, it is the extent of his persistent offending, and the nature of his relations with police, social workers and teachers, that define the habitual delinquent. The variables which determine court appearances are not simply those pertaining to the psychological state of the delinquent or even delinquent activity *per se;* they pertain also to such phenomena as levels of police activity, geographical location, social work caseloads and the cleverness (or luck) of the child in evading report and apprehension.

This discussion appears to support our previous conclusion. Intermediate treatment can be seen as a means of keeping children out of care; as a means of sustaining adolescents through a particularly difficult period of their lives; and as the negotiation and maintenance of a barrier between them and those agencies whose business is social control, and the detection and labelling of deviance. Since the medical model is associated with a situation in which residential care and training are all too frequently prescribed for persistent delinquency, this view implies, for many child-care professionals, a change in their understanding of delinquency.

Summary

It has been our intention in this chapter to summarise some contemporary views about delinquency. It goes without saying that the discussion has been highly derivative, and that no pretence is made to originality or academic competence. We have merely tried to set out what seem to us to be some of the more essential trends in delinquency theory in order that they can be used to illuminate the subsequent discussion of intermediate treatment. Three features, in particular, of delinquency have been emphasised, and, correspondingly, three broad considerations have emerged relevant to intermediate treatment. Briefly, these are:

a) The provision of new interests and activities; contact with a different environment (and, ideally, the elimination of damaging factors within that environment);
b) Group work within this framework; use of activities to provide experience of success for the young people concerned; use of activities, too, as a focus for the development of relationships and as a context for work on the pattern of norms and attitudes operating within the group.
c) The maintenance by social workers, youth workers and others of a barrier or buffer between "children in trouble" or "at risk" and the "authority agencies" – and the continued negotiation of the barrier; an effort to keep children out of care, out of the institutions which may only serve to reinforce their delinquency.

These considerations are not meant to represent anything more than broad areas of concern that may figure in the practice of intermediate treatment. They begin to suggest guide-lines, but that is all. Later on, we shall be able to see how far the projects we describe illustrate some of the points made in this chapter. But before we come to the projects, we shall take a look at the official version of intermediate treatment, as represented by D.H.S.S. publications and the regional schemes, as well as the general impression of the 1969 Act which they have, between them, created.

2 THE REGIONAL SCHEMES

Section 19 of the 1969 Children and Young Persons Act states:

> "It shall be the duty of the children's regional planning committee for each planning area . . . to make arrangements, with such persons as the committee thinks fit, for the provision by those persons of facilities for enabling directions given by virtue of section 12(2) of this Act to persons resident in the area to be carried out effectively.
>
> The committee shall specify the arrangements made in pursuance of the preceding subsection in a scheme and shall submit the scheme to the Secretary of State for him to determine the date on which it is to come into force; and the Secretary of State shall, after consultation with the committee and the relevant authorities, determine that date and notify his determination to the committee."

Although the published schemes do not represent the final shape of intermediate treatment (powers to vary them exist in accordance with section 19(4)), it can be assumed that an inspection of them will give some indication as to how the committees approached this task.

Intermediate Treatment: a guide for the Regional Planning of new forms of treatment for children in trouble was the first public statement of the Department of Health and Social Security, following transfer of responsibility for intermediate treatment to that department from the Home Office. It contained, among other things, a "dummy" scheme which has served as a model for the preparation of the regional schemes. On page 15 of this document, the following remark is made:

> ". . . It is not intended that the form in which the material in Appendix C is set out should be regarded as a standard pattern. Schemes may be presented in whatever form appears to the Regional Planning Committee to be most suitable and convenient."

Immediately after this statement, however, we find:

> "It does appear desirable, however, that there should be a degree of formality and standardisation in the way the schemes are set out."

There seems to be no way of interpreting these statements in such a way as to make them consistent with each other and it is not, therefore, surprising that, in the face of such apparently contradictory advice, the Regional Planning Committees played safe and constructed their schemes in very close initiation of the dummy in Appendix C of the D.H.S.S. booklet. The form of the dummy scheme, even more than its content, seems to have had a subtle, yet powerful, influence on the planning of intermediate treatment at the regional level.

For the most part, the schemes were compiled by working parties appointed by the Regional Planning Committees, and if the latter were unclear about the task, the working parties must have been even more so. It is evident, both by report and from an inspection of the results, that in many cases no attempt was made to lay down guidelines according to which the working parties could draw up suitable schemes even within the terms offered by the D.H.S.S. Thus each working party operated more or less independently of the others, with different criteria of selection, or no criteria at all. The final scheme, but for the addition of national facilities, was a simple aggregate of the lists prepared by the individual working parties. In the event, the working parties, too, played safe. Many of them apparently tried to locate, list and secure the co-operation of nearly every non-commercial facility already catering for young people: one finds page after page of youth clubs and centres, scout and guide troops and similar organisations. Apart from playing safe, a further motive has been suggested for this approach: the longer the list, the more impressive the scheme; and the more impressive the scheme, the more money available. For whatever reasons, the result was that the area schemes, by and large, have shown rather less imagination than the original dummy which itself is relatively free of youth clubs and scout troops, at least in the numbers in which they have since appeared in the regional plans.

The headings used to categorise intermediate treatment facilities, first set out in Appendix C, have been universally adopted by the Regional Planning Committees. They are: Name and location; Responsible person or body; Nature of facility; Sex and age-range; Conditions and procedure for admission; Times when available; Financial arrangements; Remarks. At first glance, it is rather difficult to see how this categorisation can help in the creation of a range of facilities which policy intended to span the gap between traditional supervision and residential care. In treatment terms, there is no indication of the potential location of any facility between these two extremes. The essential questions appear to be: "Where and how is the facility intermediate between supervision and care?" and "In what sense does it supply treatment?" — but answers to these questions are glaringly absent. A scheme purporting to offer varying forms of community care and treatment surely needs a framework which makes sense in policy terms; but it is in this respect that the D.H.S.S. *Guide* and the regional plans have failed radically. An alternative framework to that adopted in the regional schemes will be outlined in the concluding chapters of this book, but in the meantime we will keep to a discussion of the schemes we already have.

It must be stated here that criticism of the regional schemes is not intended as criticism of the youth service; nor is it meant to question the view that the youth service has a role to play in intermediate treatment. It will become clear that while the youth service has a role, in our opinion it is not necessarily, or exclusively, the one that has been suggested for it, nor that implied by the early literature and the area schemes.

An ironic note: it has proved, since the publication of the schemes, that many youth workers are unaware that their facilities have been included. Although one reason for this may be the time-lag between the initial preparations and the coming into effect of the schemes themselves, it also suggests a lack of consultation and discussion in the first place, at least in some instances. Meanwhile, many youth workers remain worried and suspicious about certain aspects of intermediate treatment — for example, what they see as its "compulsion" element — and unsure about the role they are supposed to be playing. Nor have the many short conferences that have taken place up and down the country done much to reassure and inform them. The result is that many of the facilities included in the regional plans, through no fault of their own, are totally unprepared for the coming of intermediate treatment. This point alone is enough to cast doubt on the usefulness of the area schemes in their present form.

In the first chapter we discussed some contemporary views of delinquency and made some very general suggestions about the forms intermediate treatment might take. We have not so far drawn explicit attention to the way in which these suggestions differ from the "official" or "popular" views of intermediate treatment, in so far as these exist at all. In the rest of this chapter, we shall discuss the pointers contained in the official publications, and in the schemes themselves, and try to bring out the central features of intermediate treatment which emerge from them, contrasting these features with the implications of what we had had to say in Chapter One.

Individuals and Groups

As we have already suggested, the official literature tends to emphasise what we have here referred to as the causes of delinquency, and the need for a form of treatment which offers a new environment, new relationships and new activities. Now, to emphasise the causes of delinquency is to focus attention, generally, on the individual, and his actions, in relation to his background, environmental and psychology. To the extent that this aspect of delinquency is emphasised to the exclusion of others, the treatment method it implies will also tend to apply to individuals — a consideration supported by the reflection that the context in any case is set by the processes of law in which proceedings are taken against, and orders made in respect of, individuals. It is likely, then, that such a treatment method will be conceived as a treatment of individuals — a point which clearly contrasts with our own insistence on group work which, whilst equally intended to support the individuals, does so in the context of a group and a particular framework of relationships.

Those anticipations are confirmed by the general impression of intermediate treatment recommendations and referrals that has been created, involving, as it does, the supervisor, the young person, and the facility to which the latter is allocated. It is reasonably clear that it is not envisaged that groups of children, whether "natural" or "artificial", will be sent to conventional youth clubs – certainly to refer such groups would be to risk the kind of trouble that some youth leaders fear. More often than not, a club will be able to accommodate one or two referrals and, in view of their already strained resources, no more. We have already indicated some of the reason for our preference for group work; this chapter may suggest why individual treatment in the context of the established youth facilities may not, in many cases, be quite so useful.

Activities

Most youth facilities seem to be broadly activity or building orientated. Our own approach to intermediate treatment suggests that this may be the wrong kind of emphasis. Whereas children may attend a local centre either to participate in some particular activity, or just as somewhere to go to meet friends and drink coffee, we have suggested that the main focus of attention in intermediate treatment should be the development of relationships between children in trouble (or at risk) themselves. This is not, of course, to say that there is no value in facilities offering the kind of service that youth clubs do; it is rather to say that, if intermediate treatment is to be a positive attempt to intervene in the behaviour and attitude patterns of children in trouble, work will have to be done that goes beyond the sort of programmes characteristically offered by many youth organisations. If, then, the conventional youth services are to play a significant role in intermediate treatment, many of them may have to review their traditional ways of working with young people (though this is not to suggest that the same may not also be true of the social services).

Some organisations, of course, are already doing just this; and it is not true that *all* youth facilities have an essentially building – or activity – centred approach. Some employ skilled group workers whose role is to attend to developing adolescent relationships, either through the medium of "talk" groups, or through activity-based groups of one kind or another. But it is fair to say that those are in a minority,, and that the above remarks will not be true of the majority of facilities included in the area schemes. Where there is this sort of provision, and this kind of skill, intermediate treatment is a viable proposition, even for individual referrals. In many cases, however, in a youth service already badly understaffed[1], it may not be.

The emphasis, in the regional schemes, on activity-based facilities again reflects the thinking in official publications. The D.H.S.S. *Guide* stresses opportunities for contact with a different environment, new activities and interests, new relationships. Leaving aside, for a moment, the question of new relationships, it is clear why this emphasis should lead to a search for established facilities already providing such opportunities. Although the *Guide* remarks that both existing and "special" facilities are acceptable, it is not surprising that the schemes should contain very few entries that amount to "special" facilities. Why should special facilities be required at all if all there is to intermediate treatment is the creation of new interests, participation in new activities and contact with a different environment? There are plenty of established facilities already providing these things for young people. It is only when further considerations are introduced – such as those we discussed under the headings of the "experience" and "identification" of delinquency – that the need for special facilities and programmes emerges.

It is such special programmes that we are concerned with, for the most part, in this book. They need not take place independently of the resources that the youth service can offer; nor are they entirely different from the ways in which some organisations are already working. But they are different from the context in which new interests and activities are offered – if they are offered – by most of the facilities included in the regional schemes.

We may add here a further point that will be taken up again later. While the schemes as a whole may reflect the "wide variety" of activities on which the D.H.S.S. booklet insists, individual facilities do not necessarily do so. This suggests a need for accurate assessment if the pattern of individual treatment referrals is adopted. The alternative, which seems far more sensible (especially in view of scepticism about assessment procedures), is to expose *each* individual, as an individual or as a member of a group, to a wide variety of activities. This exposure may itself amount to a kind of assessment, or may take place in the course of assessment. This possibility again argues for a "special" way of working in intermediate treatment which deploys community resources, as represented by the listed facilities, in a different way.

Relationships

In our view, the importance of relationships in intermediate treatment resides particularly in the form of the delinquent's association with his fellows, and, in particular, with other young people at risk, or in trouble. In the official publications, there are two main points at which relationships are mentioned or implied: (i) the requirement that there should be opportunities to develop new personal relationships, and (ii) the insistence that treatment should take place, in the main, in the company of others. It is not always very clear what point either of these requirements has. There are several possibilities, however. The D.H.S.S. stress on "new personal relationships" suggests that this opportunity is, as it were, part of the "therapy" – that the delinquent should have the opportunity to associate with new people – children, perhaps, who do not share his attitudes and norms, who have not appeared before the courts, and who may be intended to have a "good effect" on him.[2] On the other hand, there is a theme to which we have referred before, and which seems to emerge from the Home Office's *Children in Trouble* – that intermediate treatment, or intermediate treatment-type programmes, should be available to other children who may be at risk, but who have not necessarily appeared in court.[3] This is a very different matter, a question of treating other disadvantaged children from a similar environment, who have, or may be developing similar attitudes, even if they have not so far found themselves in trouble. This theme is, of course, very much in keeping with the underlying philosophy of *Children in Trouble,* which seeks to blur the distinction between "disadvantaged" and "delinquent". Interpreted in this way, the question of relationships does not have a direct bearing on the question of therapy; it has more to do with making similar opportunities available to other deprived and disadvantaged children.

Yet a third interpretation appears in the *Guide* where treatment in the company of others is represented as part of the attempt to secure the child's acceptance of treatment, an aim unlikely to be achieved "if it involves him in activities which appear to him to set him apart from his contemporaries".[4]

To make the engagement in "new personal relationships" part of the intermediate treatment therapy seems unrealistic, and may be unnecessary. From our own point of view, the possibility of relationships with children who are not in trouble or "at risk" represents something more like an objective than a technique, and depends on the young person's ability to form associations on a basis other than the norms and attitudes which characterise delinquent ties. This is something intermediate treatment can set out to achieve. One possibility would be to combine this objective with a developing interest in some activity from among the variety of activities to which a child can be exposed in the course of intermediate treatment involvement, so that he could eventually be phased into an established facility. Here he could continue to enjoy the activity, and begin to take up new relationships, hopefully undistorted by delinquent attitudes and needs.

In the case of the allocation of an individual, the extent to which there will be opportunities to form new personal relationships in the club setting will depend, of course, on the facilities elected. It is not as if only one type of child makes use of facilities of this kind. Many youth clubs already cater for children who are in the "at risk" or "in trouble" category, in which case the referrals will hardly be able to engage in associations of a kind radically different from their previous ones. Alternatively, other youth organisations may be of a type which, while they attract children other than those in this category, also, and for the same reasons, tend to deter the young people with whom we are concerned. This brings us to the next section.

A Dilemma

Any child for whom intermediate treatment is being considered may already be attached to the type of youth organisation typically represented in the scheme; or he may not be. If he is, there seems little extra to be gained by formalising the arrangement in court; if he is not, it may well be for reasons that suggest it might be pointless, or unwise, to require his attendance.

The first difficulty seems already to have been encountered in Yorkshire, where the intermediate treatment scheme came into operation in July 1973, although the number of orders made since then has been very low.[5] One reason for this is, apparently, the social workers' realisation that there is little point recommending intermediate treatment if the young person in question is already attached to the sort of youth provision listed in the schemes.[6] This is understandable, even if it could be argued that their interpretation of intermediate treatment is rather restricted (which is, of course, the point). For one thing, attachment to the facility does not seem to have prevented a court appearance; and to apply for an intermediate treatment requirement in such a case would be tantamount to asking for a simple formalisation of the attachment. It is not remarkable that supervising officers do not see much point in this. Such formalisation would hardly even amount to the stimulation of "new interests and relationships" suggested by official literature.

Parenthetically, we might note here how important positive policy decisions are, as well as channels of information and publicity. Without guidelines from the local authorities, without active discussion of the possibilities and a free exchange of ideas, intermediate treatment, as a concept, is in danger of dying a slow death in some areas. An impression of the concept is created which is so implausible that social workers are understandably reluctant to put it into practice. Alternatively, the local authority may, for various reasons, whether financial, administrative or theoretical, allow a rather uninspiring version of intermediate treatment to gain currency. It has even been suggested — to take an example mentioned earlier — that wherever possible, the most convenient facility will be used. This, as a statement of policy, hardly measures up to the principles behind the concept, even at its thinnest. The result will be, of course, not that so meaningless a procedure will actually take place, but that its evident pointlessness will end in the atrophy of the whole idea.

The second difficulty arises if the young person in question, like a substantial proportion of the juvenile population, delinquent or otherwise, is not attached to a conventional youth organisation.[7] The question is: why not? Some of the answers are not very encouraging.

To begin with, many of these young people may have been excluded from the clubs because of the very behaviour problems which bring them before the courts. Some youth workers remain very anxious about the disturbing effects such youngsters might have, in terms of damage to property and abrasive relationships with other members. A constant concern of the youth workers has been their right to reject individuals on intermediate treatment and, while no one denies them this right, it would be unfortunate if this right was frequently exercised in just those cases in which, as we believe, intermediate treatment could and should be tried. The young people most in danger of being committed into full-time care are often those that the youth clubs have most trouble with.

Perhaps a more important, and larger, category is the number of children who are themselves actively hostile to the youth service or, alternatively, totally indifferent to it. Many young people, other than those in trouble, share these attitudes, and in recent years much thought has been given to the problem of the "unclubbables" and the "unattached".[8] In some cases, this thought process has resulted in the adoption of different – sometimes radically different – approaches to work with young people. These new approaches can only be welcomed, and it is to be hoped that they can be fitted into the overall intermediate treatment framework; but it has to be said that many of the facilities listed in the regional schemes are more traditional in their styles of work. We are not suggesting, of course, that these facilities ought to change their style. Needs and preferences vary, and the youth service has to take account of them all. What we are suggesting, however, is that these facilities may not have very much to offer intermediate treatment. The delinquent system of norms and attitudes is, typically, a reactive one, at odds with the ubiquitous expectations of society and social groupings. It can be argued that much of the youth service examplifies, in a lower key, the kind of social norm against which the delinquent reacts. We find many young people, not just delinquents, rejecting youth service provision as being too much like school, too restrictive, too demanding, too unexciting.

These remarks are most obviously true of those organisations which have relatively strict codes of dress and behaviour as well as more subtle, but equally effective, restrictions of attitude, outlook and temperament; but it is also the case with organisations which, at first sight, have less structured regimes. Even the local youth club may have a particular structure of rules, etiquette and behaviour expectations which the delinquent may find, or pretend to find (which comes to the same thing), unreasonable. This, again, is understandable in view of the numbers for which such clubs have to cater, and given the personal styles of leadership amongst different club workers. But the question remains: how far can such facilities play a significant role in intermediate treatment?

It is not necessarily that the child involved in intermediate treatment will react with extreme or violent behaviour. A more likely response would be for him to dissociate, to refuse to identify with the facility and perhaps make the occasional outburst or protest. The essential problem is that the existence of certain expectations may only serve to reinforce the tension between social norms, as represented (if only in the child's mind) by the club, and the reactive norm of the delinquent – even if this tension does not emerge in extreme behaviour. For if this tension is at the root of the delinquent's attitude and behaviour pattern, to preserve it in this way can only restrict the attempt to come to grips with his problem. It may be, perhaps, that, unbeknown to the club worker, whatever happens at a superficial level inside the club, delinquent attitudes outside it will be relatively unaffected.

It must not be forgotten, either, that the reactive norm of the delinquent is, as we observed in the first chapter, connected with a basic lack of self-confidence. If he dissociates from the club situation, or reacts aggressively to it, it may simply be because he lacks the confidence to handle what can be perceived as an essentially threatening situation. In an exposed club setting, referred on an individual basis, and without the means of finding or creating an identify, he may find it very difficult to survive.

Some of these comments appear to have implications for techniques in the more protected group setting. It will be an objective both to renew the delinquent's self-confidence and to defuse what is connected with it, the tension between his reactive attitudes and conventional social norms. Self-confidence may be encouraged by the small group setting itself, where there is a chance to find an identity with a small number of young people similar to himself with the aid of a relatively high proportion of adult workers. The exposure to a variety of activities, and the opportunity to discover at least one which he enjoys and is good at, is, of course, another factor. Meanwhile, and in parallel, it may be possible to defuse the reactive attitudes by a temporary revocation of the social norms against which they are reactive – at least in terms of the visibility of imposed rules and the sanctions commonly associated with them. This, in essence, is the idea of the "democratic" group structure. If the tension between social norm and reactive attitudes can be decreased in this way – by refusing to use de facto authority to set rules, by encouraging group participation in decision-making at all levels, and by refusing to exercise, whenever possible, the sanctions which the young people will inevitably look for, provoking learning experience instead – the delinquent norm is allowed less room in which to manoeuvre and react, for there is less to react against.

There are, perhaps, two advantages to be gained from this approach. To the extent that the tension between social norms and delinquent reactions is defused, it may become possible to create other bases of association and attitude, to establish alternative foundations for self-esteem, and to the extent that the young people are no longer perceived through the structure of a given system of norms, a closer relationship and better understanding may develop between them and the adult workers. Normally, the terms on which children in trouble are encountered by adult authority figures actually get in the way of a developing relationship. This may be illustrated by social workers who operate from within an administrative or institutional structure. There are many examples of these workers encountering their clients in a setting in which these structures are either abandoned or ignored, and finding that they are able, for the first time, properly to get to know the young people, and discover things about them that could not have merged in the structured situation. The point is a simple one: if we cannot truly get to know delinquent young people, if we cannot properly understand them, there is little we can do for them as individuals, or as members of groups, or as members of a disadvantaged community.

Assessment

How are we to decide whether a child is suitable for intermediate treatment, or intermediate treatment suitable for the child? And how are we to decide which facility is best for him? On the official view of intermediate treatment, these are difficult questions.

The D.H.S.S. *Guide* required that a wide variety of facilities should be included in the regional schemes. As we observed before, the schemes, overall, do provide this variety, although individual facilities, by themselves, cannot be so comprehensive. However, the supervisor will have to be able to select just one facility from the list as most appropriate for his client. This cannot be completely satisfactory. Surely the emphasis should be not on one facility (from a wide range) for one individual, but on a wide range of facilities or activities being made available to the same person. If the child's self-esteem is an important factor in treatment, it seems desirable that he should have an opportunity to take part in as many different activities as possible so that he can find something that he enjoys or is good at. The problem of assessment resides in the fact that the social worker will not always be able to anticipate what activities these will be. Nor, for that matter, will the young person himself. Obviously, if the young person has lacked opportunity, there will be many things he will not have been able to try, and he may not know what he would like to do, or even what is available.

More generally, it can be argued that the whole social enquiry process undertaken by the supervisor cannot provide a "sufficiently detailed knowledge of the individual offender's personal and social situation to make possible a thorough and well-informed assessment".[9] If this is true, it may well prove that the intermediate treatment group can itself perform this assessment function rather better. If a small specific group can engage in a variety of activities over a period of time, with the kind of democratic atmosphere outlined at the end of the last section, the supervisor may be able to refer given individuals to established youth facilities more confidently. An appropriate facility could be chosen on the basis of what he has been able to find out about the child – and what the child has been able to find out about himself – in the course of the group's lifespan. In this sense, the distinction between the treatment itself and the assessment procedure is blurred. Within the same programme, a group may serve as a basis for work with its members, and as a basis for assessing them, so that they will be able to pass on to further activities and organisations later.[10] And unlike assessment for residential care, which is usually static and short-term, with a distinct cut-off point when the child moves out to his placement, assessment in the intermediate treatment group would allow for individual development over an indefinite period.

Supervision

The role of the supervisor, in this account, is by implication a fairly active one. This is a further contrast with the general impression of intermediate treatment that has been created by the schemes. With the supervisor's role apparently restricted to referral and liaison, he need only locate, assess and secure the co-operation of a suitable facility, and refer the client to it. At this point, so it has sometimes seemed (and as it has frequently been stated), the main responsibility is the youth worker's: the supervisor's statutory duty to "advise, assist and befriend" is virtually delegated to him. On some occasions (at conferences, for example), youth workers have insisted, on their own account, that the supervisor should "stop at the door", and not actually interfere with treatment. But this approach seems unhelpfully to isolate intermediate treatment from the child's other experiences, at home and in the community, with which, theoretically at least, the supervisor is more familiar. As we shall see in the next two chapters, more active supervisor involvement in the group situation seems to be both desirable and effective. Intermediate treatment ought ideally to be a comprehensive method of social work, intervening on a number of levels in a co-ordinated and systematic treatment programme which would be at least as effective as residential care. If the agent of statutory supervision does not participate in this programme, it may even be possible for the treatment agency itself to engage in supervision and casework. This is what happens with some of the projects described in this book.

Conclusions

In this chapter we have criticised that view of intermediate treatment which would see the youth organisations playing their conventional role. Briefly: if intermediate treatment is to be an attempt to combat a problem that is worth combatting, then we think it doubtful whether this conventional role has much to offer, especially if the relation between facility and supervisor is one of liaison only, rather than supervisor participation. In general terms, the youth service can be understood as having a preventive role, in so far as social education of young people is one of the service's primary aims. Even in these terms, however, two qualifications are necessary. In the first place, social education is not something of which only parts of the juvenile population are in need: it is surely something we try to provide for all children, delinquent or not. Ideally, then, the youth service task is to reach all children – in some context or another – and help them in some of the more difficult aspects of growing up. But it does not seeem that this task is one which can be harnessed to court proceedings, just because it is an objective which applies universally. Rather, the youth services themselves must be ready to reach out in different ways – ways which may resemble conventional methods only slightly – in order to make contact with young people who have rejected traditional forms of youth work. In any case, only a small proportion of young people are actively engaged in the traditional forms of youth provision, a fact that has led to the experiments in detached youth work and work based on the perception of certain needs and meanings rather than centred on a particular building or a pro-set form of life. We believe that this style of work is a more realistic model for youth work involvement in intermediate treatment, and this belief may reflect the ethos of those youth workers who see in the "official" view of intermediate treatment something contrary to the spirit of youth work, and who see the youth service as a resource for young people rather than a demand on them.

As it is, however, we have intermediate treatment, and we have the area schemes; we have individuals receiving orders from the courts and we have conventional youth facilities waiting to receive them; we have the requirement, on the one hand, that money under the 1969 Act is available only as a result of court proceeedings, and we have the further requirement that it is available only if the facility used is listed in the regional schemes. While intermediate treatment will have to begin by conforming to these requirements, it is conceivable that ways will be found of getting round them. Some authorities have already arranged to combine 1969 Act funds with money available under other legislation, notably the 1963 Act. It may also become possible, in a similar way, to ignore the requirement of court proceedings (which is, in any case, the strongest argument against involving in intermediate treatment children who have not committed offences). If these developments occur, and if the movements in the youth service, described in the previous paragraph, continue, it is conceivable that a fruitful merging of styles and objectives will take place. The kind of work with groups that we see as the best option in intermediate treatment, and youth work based on community situations and perceived needs, will begin to resemble each other more and more, both as regards their methods and techniques, and in virtue of what they are trying to do. It may even be that intermediate treatment will be one of the stimuli needed to provoke new developments in youth work, and encourage those that are already under way. Intermediate treatment may then become a style of working – not a piece of legislation – in an area which is currently the domain neither of the conventional youth service nor of the social services, and into which both can move in a generic way.

One danger, however, will have to be avoided. It seems that in some social services departments, where social workers have, understandably, rejected the regional schemes as worthless, there has been a tendency to go it alone, independently of those organisations which have the facilities and expertise to help. This is unfortunate. It is not as if rejecting the area schemes means rejecting the youth services themselves. But this is what may happen. In intermediate treatment there is the possibility of a new, or extended, concept of work with the disadvantaged young which is currently the province neither of the youth service nor of social services, though both operate on its margins, as do the education department and the probation service. All the services have expertise and resources which work in this area will require, though further experience will suggest other requirements and needs. It will be unfortunate if a certain over-lapping does not take place and if a more generic style cannot emerge from their co-operation, even if this requires an experimental and developmental period during which the services edge towards each other across a gap which, for the time being, none can bridge alone.

In the meantime, transitional models of interaction be worked out in order to accommodate the various styles of work that can take place now. The form of group work we have already discussed, and which will be analysed in later chapters, is one such style, though it is not the only one. Even if the conventional use of youth service facilities is rejected, the adoption of even this style does not mean that no use at all can be made of these facilities, or of youth service personnel, expertise, buildings and equipment. A theoretical and administrative framework in which all these elements can be combined will be worked out in chapters seven and eight.

What, then, finally, of the regional schemes? We are rather sceptical. Very few of the facilities listed in them are being used, and we would hope that the resources they have to offer would not necessarily be used in a conventional way when they are. Meanwhile, the schemes themselves provide a lot of people with time-consuming work which might be better spent on other things: supervisors and intermediate treatment officers have, in many cases, duty to liaise with listed facilities, while the Regional Planning Committees have, in the course or rather academic discussion, to amend the lists themselves, deciding whether to include or reject various facilities when the real point seems to be, not the acceptance or rejection of items in a catalogue, but the assessment of actual treatment programmes. Perhaps those who have suggested withdrawing most of the facilities listed in their own area schemes have a point; perhaps, in the final analysis, the regional schemes, in the present form, should be abandoned altogether.

3 TEN PROJECTS: DESCRIPTIONS

If the regional schemes and the conventional youth service do not, as we have argued, provide suitable models for intermediate treatment, we must look elsewhere. In this chapter, some projects which have developed different approaches are described. Some of these projects came into being as a result of the initiative taken by the Department of Health and Social Security with twelve local authorities (written up in the booklet. *Intermediate Treatment Project.*[1]) Others were also set up by local authorities as specific intermediate treatment facilities which could explore the possibilities of the 1969 Act. Three of the projects had been in existence for some time before, and came to be seen as possible forms of intermediate treatment when the concept was introduced by *Children in Trouble.* With one exception, the accounts that follow were either submitted directly by project leaders or abstracted, with their approval, from lengthier reports. The exception, as already explained, is Dallington Lodge, in whose case description is restricted to outline proportions.

The Albany Scheme, Lewisham

This project began in August 1971 with the aim of establishing provision appropriate for children and young people who would be the subjects of supervision orders with an intermediate treatment requirement. The area chosen for the project was Deptford, the part of Lewisham which produces the highest number of child-care referrals and juvenile court appearances, though with a relatively high level of community action amongst tenants associations and other interest groups. The Albany, a community work agency in the area, has been instrumental in helping many of these groups to organise and achieve their objectives. Although the project was initiated by Lewisham Social Services, then, it could not, being based at the Albany, be perceived as something too directly connected with the department, or with the police and courts.

Initially, the project's aims were:

To enhance the quality of the participants' primary relationships by supporting them in their interactions with peer groups and adult workers.

To minimise negative and destructive behaviour by supporting positive behaviour and helping participants to deal with feelings at a verbal level.

To encourage the participants to support and help one another through this verbalisation.

To minimise delinquency and truancy by facilitating significant recreational and social activities.

To give sufficient support within the community to ensure that the children do not have to be taken into residential care.

To put participants in touch with a youth serving agency in which they might play an increasingly important part.

To put the participants in touch with appropriate educational and vocational opportunities.

The first group was made up of referrals from the district social services office and consisted of boys of similar age and circumstances (being from large and effectively fatherless families, and attending the same school). It was intended that sessions should eventually take place in the school itself, but to begin with, eight sessions were conducted at the Albany. It was hoped that these first sessions would see the beginnings of a relationship between group members and workers, and that some of the more extreme testing out of the situation would have been worked through before the move into the school. The programme at the Albany included model-making, cooking, football and rough games; there were also two trips out to the swimming pool and bowling alley. Use of video equipment was also arranged.

When the group did move into the school, for sessions in the afternoon lasting about two hours, tensions were created as the boys began to play social workers and teachers against each other. Attempts to explain the differing expectations and limitations of behaviour in the school and at the Albany were met with hostility, and confusion about roles and relationships in the two different settings extended to the workers as well as the group members. The situation was relieved by taking the group's video equipment "on location", and away from the school altogether. The group terminated its school-based programme after three months.

This experience indicated, among other things, that three months was a very short time in the life of such a group, and that anxiety caused by its imminent termination was an inhibiting factor. It was decided that later groups would be based at the Albany, and an open-ended arrangement was adopted whereby the point of termination would not be defined. The idea was to create a situation in which referrals could be made over a longer period, with participants leaving the group when it had served its purpose. This has meant in practice, periods of involvement ranging from two to eighteen months. At the same time, the project leader remained interested in running groups in association with local schools.

Another school group consisted of boys referred by the Head of the lower school of a local comprehensive, and was made up of West Indian boys, again from effectively fatherless families. It differed from the first group in that sessions were conducted, from the start, as lessons during normal school time (the course being called "Learning about Ourselves"), and that the boys had been posing behaviour problems in school. Each session was limited to half an hour per week, though on eight occasions, an entire afternoon was taken up by a trip out. In addition, there was one full day trip, one evening trip, and one weekend at a youth hostel. In all the group lasted two terms. Sessions set out to encourage verbal interaction amongst participants, and from the beginning discussions were steered towards areas in which the boys might be experiencing difficulties — for example, the kind of contribution they were expected to make at home.

The "talk sessions", however, tended to be unrelated to the activity programmes out of school, and in two later groups, an effort was made to relate the two more — to find an activity which automatically threw up questions about relationships and feelings, so that these questions could be examined in a way that seemed purposeful to the group. A local adult training centre for the mentally handicapped had a football team whose trainer/manager, who was also the woodwork instructor, was looking around for schoolboys to help in the training sessions. It was arranged that the two groups should go to the centre once a week for separate sessions, and that on rainy days the boys could spend the time helping out in the woodwork shop. This gave an opportunity of face-to-face contact with another group, and provided a situation in which a skill the most of the boys possessed (football) could be brought into play. Beyond this, it provided a situation in which the boys could enter into relationships with people who were very unlike themselves. Fears that the boys' response to the people at the cente would be one of fear, derision or rejection, have proved unfounded.

One of the groups was made up of boys in the last year of the lower school (13-14 years of age), while the other was drawn from the fourth and fifth years (15-16). The younger group, seven boys in all, was recruited according to criteria similar to those used in the formation of the previous group, while for the older group, the Head recommended all the participants in the first group, many of whom had found the transition from the lower school so difficult that their attendance had dropped off.

The majority of the boys in the scheme seem to have gained in competence and confidence, and staff at the school have suggested that the movement observed in the group was also visible in behaviour in the classroom, particularly in the case of boys who were notably withdrawn.

Dallington Lodge, Northampton

Dallington Lodge was established by Northamptonshire Social Services Department in 1971 as a specialist intermediate treatment centre. It is financed by the local authority, though in policy and methods it is independent. Set up as a specialist provision for young people at risk who were unable to make use of ordinary youth facilities, it has experimented with various forms of work within the framework of the 1969 Act. It is housed in extensive premises located in a very residential area, although there is a close contact with a nearby housing estate, which the centre sees, and local schools. Several different types of group work are being employed.

There is, firstly, "short-term residential treatment". Groups of young people (up to twelve, and with a fairly limited age range) spend brief periods in residence at the Lodge – either weekends, or block weeks. These periods are spread over nine months or a year, and meet the 30-day requirement of the Act. Activities available include outdoor pursuits. When young people are in residence for a week, they continue to attend school from the centre.

Groups of up to 15 children (again with specific age ranges) meet weekly at the centre in "activity groups", although similar groups, administered by the centre, are also being set up in various youth centres in Northampton, staffed by youth club workers. The Lodge groups meet for sessions during school holidays, too, and are also involved in residential sessions and camps occasionally. Outdoor challenge activities have been used with some young people, though always in the context of relationships already established with centre staff. These have been limited to groups of up to ten, which have participated in camping, youth hostelling and have visited an adventure centre.

A more recent addition is a "school unit" which provides out of school education for individuals and groups of children who are not able to make full use of normal schooling because of social or family problems. The centre also runs playgroups and a mother and baby group.

The centre staff team consists of a warden, a domestic bursar and the school unit teacher, though it will eventually include a deputy warden/group worker and a social worker. The team is supported by a number of paid part-time workers and volunteers: all meet regularly for planning and assessment sessions in the case of all residential and day groups. The warden has begun to play an increasingly large part in statutory supervision, although direct contact with families was, in the first instance, limited, and this aspect of the work, involving a social worker engaged in family casework and family group work, is now seen as an inherent part of the overall treatment plan.

Eastern Ravens Trust, Stockton-on-Tees

The Eastern Ravens Youth Club was started in 1961 by one voluntary leader, working in a socially deprived area of Stockton-on-Tees. From the start, the founder had close contact with others (for example, school teachers, clergy, Children's Department and Probation) who knew the area and its people, but it was some years before there were any other regular youth club leaders helping him.

In 1966, the original leader was given a year's leave by his employers to develop the club. The Education Department agreed to pay him as a full-time leader, and the work expanded considerably as more voluntary leaders became interested. The full-time work was then continued by Community Service Volunteers until 1969, when the Education

Department created the post of full-time Youth Leader, and the first qualified youth leader was appointed.

The emphasis in Eastern Ravens has always been on voluntary leadership and there are currently about 20 adults working in the Club, mostly unqualified, but some with part-time youth work training. There is also a part-time secretary, a club van, and three sets of premises. The first is a large converted terrace house, which contains club rooms, the office and leader accommodation. The second is a converted public toilet used as a club room for younger groups. The third is a lonely, partially derelict farmhouse on the edge of the North Yorkshire Moors, which is being renovated by club members and is used mainly for weekend camps.

From the start, Eastern Ravens has been a closed club with membership by invitation. Most of the youth work is done in small groups (5-8 children with one or two adults) with the expectation that each group will continue for several years. The first group was formed when the members were aged 10, and normally the starting age is 8-11. Regular visiting of members' homes and general involvement in the local community is seen as a vital part of the work, and in the last two years this has expanded, with the running of holiday play programmes and the designation of part of the area as a Government Improvement Area.

Eastern Ravens works with boys and girls from a deprived and delinquent background. The aim is to meet their basic needs for self-identity, love, and security and self-esteem, in ways that their home environment will not. The emphasis in the group work is therefore on (a) consistent relationships, with adult leaders and each other, and (b) increased experience of places, people, situations, and ideas. When a group is formed, members are selected in consultation with as many knowledgeable workers as possible (schools, social workers, Probation Service), and if the young people agree to join the group, they cannot then opt out unilaterally, since the leader will maintain contact by home visiting, and try to attract the individual back into the group.

Normally each group meets once a week, with perhaps one weekend and one week camping or holidaying together during the year. In addition, there may be crises with particular individuals, such as family illness, court appearances, etc., in which club leaders will be involved. The group continues to meet until its members are about 14, when it normally breaks up because of the growing independence of the youngsters. However, work with them on an individual basis can continue, and this generally occurs with those exhibiting greatest needs. The leaders then move to being caseworkers, and this relationship can, and sometimes does, continue indefinitely. Another method, often complementary to casework, is to have a more open youth club of age-range 14-18, consisting of ex-group members and their friends, again meeting once a week, with regular weekend activities as well.

In addition to this intensive work with groups and individuals, Eastern Ravens is broadly involved in the local community. This is done formally by means of running a football team, summer camps for non-group members, and play schemes, and informally by contacts with residents, schools and social workers. The Club has initiated or supported local community action when this seemed appropriate. Through these many contacts, there is a general awareness of the needs of individuals, and potential group members can be noted. In general, of course, there are far more candidates than there are leaders to work with them, even though the Club operates only in a small area of Stockton-on-Tees.

Currently, the annual budget of Eastern Ravens is:

Group activities	£800	This is for an official club membership of 80, with approximately another 120 children with whom Eastern Ravens does some work (family visits, summer camps).
Van	£700	
Property	£600	
Administration	£800	
Leaders training	£100	
Total	£3000	

The money is raised as follows:

Local authority grant aid:	£1400	In addition, the leader's salary is paid by the local authority.
Covenants	£250	
Donations	£800	
Fund-raising activities	£300	
Rent from property	£250	
Total	£3000	

With this background of youth work amongst delinquents, Eastern Ravens has been involved in discussions on Teesside about Intermediate Treatment since 1972. Although it is possible to view normal club activities as intermediate treatment, it was decided to modify the traditional working methods somewhat, and to put forward a separate scheme to the Regional Planning Committee. In 1973, this was approved, the basis being a group of 8 boys, aged 11-13, meeting for 26 weeks, with additional weekend activities. However, no court orders were made until 1974, and in fact most of these candidates did not meet the original criteria of the scheme, being either the wrong age, or living some distance from the club. In the end, a group of 4 boys, aged 11-14, began meeting in April 1974, with 2 adult leaders. The most obvious difference from other Eastern Ravens groups are that it began when members were older, that its time-span is fixed, and that the 'Community Work' support system of the Club is not available to most of the group members, or their families, since they live outside the area in which the Club normally operates.

These are all disadvantages, when comparing the likely effectiveness of the intermediate treatment group to other Eastern Ravens groups. However, it is too early to say that the disadvantages are necessarily serious, or that even so the group work will be ineffective. It is fair to say that neither Eastern Ravens, nor Teesside Social Services Department, had anticipated that it would be so difficult to set up the first group. This first scheme is experimental and a full report will be issued after six months, so that the lessons learned can be incorporated into future intermediate treatment groups.

Haylands Junior Club, Bedford

This club originated from the request of the Home Office Children's Section that Bedfordshire Children's Department should produce a project for intermediate treatment. The Youth Service readily agreed to the use of their youth club premises when a Youth Leader, advising on the project, suggested the use of his club and personal help.

Haylands began in February 1971, and has some 79 boys referred to it, 12 of whom have subsequently been committed to care, while five have been made the subject of supervision orders. The club is staffed by the youth leader, a senior social worker, two other social workers, and as many students as possible from local colleges. Boys aged between 10 and 14 are referred by social agencies, probation, and existing members. The Juvenile Liaison Bureau also made nominations.

Club members are transported to and from the Club by a worker bus and social worker cars. The club's sweet shop is open and a 'pop' drink is provided free under section 1 of the 1963 C.Y.P.A. The club meets from 5.00. p.m. to 6.30. p.m. on a Wednesday, has had two annual camps, a weekend camp and day trips. Football, basketball, cricket, badminton, draughts, darts, skittles, cards, chess and scrabble have all been played. Table football and table tennis are always available. Average attendance is 17 out of 25 members at any one time. The club came to the end of its first cycle of members in October 1973, and at that time the average length of membership was about 20 months. Eleven had been members for over 24 months and 6 were founder members. The second cycle of members are younger and many have referred themselves although their families have previously been known to Social Services.

The aims of the club are:

To prevent delinquency by 10-14 year old boys at risk who live within an urban area of 70,000.

To reduce boredom by introducing socially accepted forms of interest and activity.

To develop status and skill as aids to maturity and a sense of personal worth.

To introduce the discipline of club life and an appreciation of its value, in the hope that the boys will progress to ordinary youth clubs at 14. (Most of the boys come from the main delinquent areas of the town; without help and guidance they acquire such destructive attitudes as to make them either unacceptable to clubs at the age of 14, or incapable of benefitting by attending).

To introduce a more positive experience of adult supervision and help than is usually available within large organisations, disturbed home situations, or in contacts with authority figures such as police and social workers.

To assess and work with each individual boy's strength and weakness in his relationship with his peers, parents, and other authority figures.

It has been very difficult to keep regular staff interested and sharing the aims of the Club. There have been three changes of youth leader and the social workers tend to change every other year, if not more frequently. Naturally, most of the time taken up by the club is in overtime, and few social workers can afford to take time off on another occasion. It has been very difficult to bring those referring boys, those working with them in the club, and those interested in the development of the Club together, although three monthly meetings have been attempted.

There have been a few aggressive outbursts by individuals. However, these appear to relate to the life of the group rather than to individual needs. There was a particularly aggressive period in which considerable damage was achieved by the group when the staff had changed and the co-ordination and thought between the staff was at its worst. This aggression and damage took the form of disruptive behaviour, personal attacks on boys who appeared natural scapegoats, damage to transport, etc. An improvement in the co-ordination of staff and in a sharing of aims and information reduced this element considerably.

One of the ideas of the Club was to get the boys to realise that their ideas were important and that what went on in the club was very much their responsibility. Regular meetings were tried originally, but it was found that the more disruptive elements attempted to avoid these meetings and refused to come. A compromise was reached in which it was made clear to all members that their ideas are welcome at any time, and that specific meetings are held when there is an event or happening in the Club which needs to be discussed.

It was gradually realised in the early days that more and more concentration was being put into organising sporting events and that the more withdrawn boys were not engaging in these activities. It has therefore been possible to develop a considerable number of activities for the withdrawn who seek the one-to-one relationship and the one-to-one expertise. Chess has been one of the main ways in which this has been achieved, though painting, drawing and draughts have also been used.

The attachments which some of the older boys formed for the Club produced a problem in that the growing stability of the club precluded the admission of others urgently needing attention. The raising of the school leaving age removed the natural break with the Club so that an artificial one had finally to be agreed upon which is regarded as their fourteenth birthday unless there is some over-riding reason why they should continue. This has produced resentment and feelings of rejection.

The first cycle of boys did not join the older clubs when the time came for them to leave. It was originally supposed that because they met in a professionally led youth club which they could join when they were fourteen, they would naturally go on to this club where the leader was one of those they had known at Haylands. This did not prove a sufficient incentive. It was thought that if they were to become interested in a particular activity, boxing, for example, it would then be possible to transfer them. This was tried over a period of eight weeks, but despite the initial promise shown by a number of boys, none of them continued their membership once the transport facility was withdrawn, and one of the club's leaders ceased to attend. Nor was an attempt to form boys into small groups which could be latched on to other clubs successful. In the end, the boys were told that they had a certain amount of time, once they became fourteen, to adjust to the idea of going to a senior club. Membership of the club which they chose would be paid for a year, and there would be a short overlapping period of membership of both clubs. They originally leapt at this idea, but none continued in membership of senior clubs even so.

The problem of colour in this multi-racial club is quite containable in the normal club sessions, but has got out of hand on the annual camps and not been dealt with effectively then. Tensions within the residential group seemed to make this a natural divide and a means of scapegoating.

There has been an almost total lack of involvement of supervisors other than those who are committed to the club as weekly helpers. There has been very little feedback or even requests for feedback from the Probation Service, for example. The idea that these officers should drop in and share activities has not been taken up by them. Supervisors have said that their children have benefitted when asked directly, but have not been very specific about this. It is, however, interesting to note that those nominated by the Juvenile Liaison Officers dropped out as they had no regular supervision, although those who were nominated, but whose supervisors did not participate, still continued to come.

There has been a failure in the club to bridge the gulf that exists between those children who are in case and those who are not. Originally, the club included boys from a local children's home, but these all left within a very short time. The 12 boys who have been committed to care all remain interested in the club and ask about it when they see the officers involved. However, with only one exception, they have failed to continue attending the club once committed, even though it has been possible for a number of them. There appears to be a mark upon them which stops them wanting to face their fellows after they have been committed to care.

The club has, however, been instrumental in giving an identity of significance to a number of boys. They have adopted roles within the club which they have appreciated and been proud of. One boy always protected the newcomers, another provided the music for weekly sessions, another became chess champion . . . and so on. They very much see themselves as Haylands Junior Club, and see themselves as a privileged group. They have shown considerable loyalty to the organisation over and above that which they appear to show anything or anyone else. The weekly attendance is much above that of an ordinary youth club in proportion, and the length of contact that these boys who come from unsettled backgrounds have established with the club is remarkable.

A larger number of the boys have become increasingly aware of their effect on others and aware of the effect that certain behaviour has on the group through examination of what has happened in the club and what effect some boys' attendance has on it. Even the most disruptive boy in the club was able to think about another boy who was away from home. He was able to relate this to his own experience.

The boys have seen another dimension of those who supervise them. The supervisors have gained respect from the boys' parents who know that they can share with the worker problems of control and behaviour. Magistrates have been impressed with the knowledge that workers have of certain boys, through their involvement in the club, and have given more weight to their recommendations as a result. The major achievement has probably been with those boys who have subsequently come into care: they did so a lot more willingly and trustingly because of what they experienced in the club.

There may be an argument against bringing a group of boys with similar needs and delinquent attitudes together in this way. But inspection of the kind of youth clubs being proposed for intermediate treatment shows that their staffing ratios tend to be 1:15 or 1:20 – and clearly these boys could not survive. The loyalty the boys have shown the club would appear to prove that they need it, and that they can identify with it and acquire skill and confidence in association with it. There is still, however, a question as to whether the expensive means justify this end.

Higher Clarence, Teesside

In 1970, Teesside's Children's Department accepted the invitation of the D.H.S.S. Development Group to explore the needs for, and the facilities available to, Intermediate Treatment. After surveying the range of youth facilities available, the Port Clarence-Haverton Hill area was selected as the most suitable location for a project. The area illustrates many aspects of cultural poverty and environmental poverty, being designated a category 'D' area in the early 1960s. A run-down of population was expected, leading to final residential clearance. The area's only youth facility, which had met on the same premises as a fairly modern social club, closed down shortly after the intermediate treatment group started when its only leader had a serious accident.

The Children's Department, and later the Social Services Department, were responsible for the establishment of groups and for their financial support. A grant was available for the payment of rent, purchase of materials, and to cover the costs of visits. Transport was also made available when requested. Co-ordination was undertaken by the Assistant Children's officer, but the detailed planning and development of the project was clearly the responsibility of the leaders. There were problems relating to increasing the number of permanent social worker leaders and the project became rather overdependent on student leadership.

The original objectives were set out when the group started, and were probably over-ambitious. They were later modified and particularised. They are, however, relevant, as they influenced the important early stages of the group's development:

To provide interest and stimulus for children living in a rather depressing area, often in large families, some with definite home problems. To provide a close and consistent enough relationship for members to identify with one or more leaders and to be influenced in their social learning by this. To try to provide situations and experiences which will at the same time provide help and support, and an opportunity of learning appropriate behaviour, which can be transferred to their life outside the group. To create an atmosphere of trust, in which individual children can bring a problem to the leader and receive understanding help.

The group was established in a fairly close-knit and relatively isolated area. It was decided at the outset to restrict membership to the area within one mile of the centre, and also to limit numbers so that the staff-child ratio would not exceed 1:4. In effect, two groups were set up, a younger group (8-11) with an average membership of 15, and a slightly older group (11-13) with an average membership of 12.

Most of the original 15 children were referred from families under voluntary supervision. To increase numbers, each child was invited to bring on other friend from the immediate community. In the early stages, and especially when the youth club closed, it was difficult to restrict membership as many children wanted to join. Eventually changes of membership took place, and after 20 months, approximately 50% of the membership had changed. Despite regular meetings with social workers in the area, only one or two of the later arrivals were referrals. Periodic meetings with social workers who had referred children were arranged and a two-way channel of information and assessment was valuable. This was not, however, frequent enough or structured enough to allow a joint planning of casework and intermediate treatment, and none of the group leaders were directly involved in casework of the families represented.

It was planned at the outset that the groups should operate on an unstructured, fairly permissive basis which allowed a degree of freedom and lack of inhibition, both in relationships between members and in those with leaders. This also meant that the leaders and property were exposed at times to fairly strong acting-out behaviour. Members of the local community reinforced the leaders' awareness that the building was not theirs and restrictions which were necessary were often imposed for this reason.

The enthusiastic response of members to activities and visits which took them out of their environment was more significant in relation to the first of the objectives listed earlier than any strong commitment to new interests or activities within the group's base. The introduction of such activities as art, modelling and free drama was received with initial enthusiasm, but new interests were rarely sustained for more than two or three sessions. Attempts were made to involve the group in planning programmes, but suggestions were usually limited to experiences already enjoyed, or were sometimes impractical, given the time and resources available. Discussion of the possibilities was not within the experience of the children, and usually a straight vote was taken where more than one suggestion was made. After the first six months, with the younger group in particular, an attempt was made to focus a part of each session on a central activity in which all members could join, as well as allowing free choice for remaining time. For this, however, more planning and control by leaders was required.

Each group met weekly for approximately one and a half hours. This was varied according to the needs of the programme, and usually visits and activities away from the centre lasted considerably longer. In addition, a number of longer visits were arranged, taking up a whole day or weekend, or during school holidays; the older group had two camping weekends.

The groups were started as a pilot project in November 1970, and at that time, no definite limit was set, though it was envisaged that if successful the project might be developed as a facility within the regional plan. Apart from one or two children, who were under the minimum age, no child was excluded from the group, and only one boy was removed by the courts on a care order. There was a natural turn-over of membership, but about half of the members in July 1972 had been in the groups for 18 months.

Considering the limited time available, quite close and significant relationships developed between several children and particular leaders. This was evidenced most clearly by the negative reactions of certain children to the departure of a particular leader. The need for stable leadership or the matching of the group's duration with leaders' ability was a lesson learned from this project.

The project experienced a certain amount of resentment and disapproval from members of the community whose children were not involved in the groups, and from some members of the management committee of the centre. The latter were afraid of the wear and tear on their premises, and attempts by the leaders to encourage the re-opening of the youth club were not enthusiastically received. Although a good relationship with local junior schools was established, the secondary school, three miles away, remained more sceptical of the group's objectives and methods.

Islington Family Service Unit Intermediate Treatment Centre

The project was set up in September 1971, under the auspices of the

Islington Family Service Unit with the support of the Inner London Education Authority, who paid for one teacher for the project, and the Islington Social Services Department through whom the Centre received an Urban Aid Grant covering other staff costs and all running expenses. A short-life terrace house, provided on licence by the Islington Council, was adapted for use as the Centre, and groundwork was done with the two schools involved in the project.

The Centre opened with a staff of three – two teachers and a social worker – and five children, but has expanded to include six staff members and up to 15 children. The age range of the children is 12 to 15½. They attend the Centre from 9.30 a.m. to 3.30 p.m., Monday to Thursday, throughout normal school terms. Average attendance is about 90%, varying between 100% and 65% for best and worst attendance. Attendance is supported during a child's first weeks and at crisis times by daily collection, but children come unaided about 75% of the time.

Children are referred by the school where it feels that the Centre might provide a suitable service for a problem pupil The referral is supported by a report from Educational Welfare and supplement by reports from Child Guidance and Social Services, if they are involved. Centre staff always meet a child and the family before he or she is accepted at the Centre: the family must be stable enough for it to be possible to work with the child in relation to a consistent environment. The majority of the children at the Centre tend to be withdrawn and isolated non-attenders, although the first group contained two aggressive exceptions. They seem to benefit from the small numbers and the more informal atmosphere in which they can overcome some of their fears about confrontations with authority, the inability to learn successfully, and their difficulties in relation to a large peer-group, where they feel threatened. With one exception, all had extremely poor attendance records of under 30% in the school term prior to their starting at the Centre.

The working day at the Centre is split into three periods. The morning contains two periods of an hour and a quarter length each. This allows time for a subject to be explored in depth, with reasonable time for discussion and practical work. The afternoon session begins at 1.30 and, in contrast to the fairly high pressure work periods of the morning, is given over to more informal, creative or recreational activities: art on Mondays, a visit (recreational or education) on Tuesdays, sport on Wednesdays, hobby periods on Thursdays. A variety of projects has been developed, ranging from woodwork and painting to needlework and gardening. Cookery for both boys and girls has proved popular. The afternoon sessions have allowed for a tremendous acceleration of creative skills. Self-consciousness and inhibition have given way to a less formalised, more imaginative style, and a greater freedom of expression.

Lessons take place in two mixed ability, mixed age, groups of seven, with never more than four staff members on duty at any one time, the fourth being available if children are being taken into school, or if there is individual or family crisis. The high staff-child ratio enables a considerable degree of personal attention, and with the understanding and dissolution of learning blocks, the children become less afraid of expressing their ignorance in a particular field. This enables them to begin to appreciate the learning process itself as well as the subject matter contained. Where lack of written ability has been a hindrance to natural expression, the use of tape-recorder and typewriters have helped to overcome inhibiting learning blocks.

Holiday visits to a youth hostel have also taken place, with the aid of a mini-bus bought out of Centre funds. The first of these visits provided a definite cohesion of group identity, and a greater confidence in members' ability to exist outside the family environment. The second reinforced developing group awareness, and allayed fears of individual challenge in the conduct of new activities, outside the children's range of normal experience.

Initially, Fridays were left free for the preparation of the following week's time-table, and for the necessary liaisons between Centre, home and school. It allowed time for other administrative duties and for preparation of modifications to the premises. As the group's confidence increased, however, informal visits were made to the Centre, the children busying themselves in whatever projects they were interested in, and discovering that the business of the Centre's administration was a reasonable process in which they themselves could be involved. With the arrival of a full-time Community Service Volunteer, visits became more frequent on Saturdays, when help was given in the cleaning of the premises and in preparation of the class-room. In this way the relationship with the Centre was stabilised, outside of the formal schooling structure.

Increasingly, the Centre has been involved in activities outside those which take place during school hours, becoming something of a community resource. It has taken on the role of a base to which children can return at times of crisis, a role which implies recognition of the fact that the problems children express during the school day cannot be separated from the rest of their lives. The use of the Centre in this way includes overnight accommodation, as well as the permanent availability of staff members for discussion and advice. The Centre is also used as a meeting place for group members who find their home situations claustrophobic, or feel unable to invite their friends home.

The expanding role of the Centre reflects the lack of provision for this age group in the area. During the halfterm period of the Spring term in 1973, the Centre was open to anyone prepared to become involved in one of the projects organised by the CSVs – silk-screen printing and the renovation of an unused basement. The projects themselves were of little importance, but several members of the Centre group turned up and 15-20 other teenagers. The CSVs also opened a youth club on the premises – the only one in the immediate area – at which projects were offered to the children through volunteers with specific skills, and in which a disco also figured. The membership of this club eventually stabilised at about 30, and began to take its own initiatives. The only workable foundation for the club's activities has proved to be a social one that is credible in terms of locality. Many of the members have been described as "unclubbable" in that they find themselves unable to fit into the smooth running regime of the regular youth club.

The Centre began by seeing the reintegration of the children into the school as an important objective. The first attempt to achieve this, however, with a brother and sister, failed when the children's confidence deteriorated into fear and reluctance and, eventually, panic-stricken non-attendance, despite the time spent with them by Centre staff. This damaged the group's security at the Centre and lowered morale about the possibility of returning to school successfully. The Centre responded to this failure by developing links with the schools more energetically, and involving some school staff in the life of the Centre. Both schools involved offered participation in certain lessons by groups of children from their own school, and two teachers made regular visits to the Centre. But both schools turned down the proposal of the "half-way house" facility inside the school. However, an arrangement was made with one school that the whole Centre, pupils and staff, should visit once a week for a period of art, and a joint project was initiated, using video equipment, on the basis of once-a-week meetings at the Centre. This involved Centre children in the dynamics of a larger group in which their relationships with the children from the school would be qualitatively different from the close relationships at the Centre, or their social relationships out of school. Though total co-operation was not achieved, a nucleus did form within the group, and video equipment emerged as a useful medium well worth exploiting.

The experience at the Centre has led the staff to reflect that "ideally, the schools should be able to offer an environment which is attractive and relevant to the needs of all; all truancy is, in part, a rejection of what school is offering, and it is not such a small problem that it can be ignored as being merely an abnormal response by the emotionally disturbed or immature . . . the most important lesson which can be learned . . . if truancy is to become a decreasing rather than an increasing problem, is the value of small informal groups as a focus for both the intellectual and emotional development of individuals."

Northorpe Hall, Mirfield (Yorkshire)

The Northorpe Hall Trust aims at enabling boys to live well-adjusted and law-abiding lives in their own families. To achieve this, it operates an intensive family casework service within the boys' homes and invites the boys for regular weekend visits, in groups, to Northorpe Hall. All that is possible is done to strengthen any beneficial ties that the boys may have within their home environment.

Currently, a boy attends Northorpe for ten weekends in each year, in addition a ten-day holiday and possible extra weekends in times of crisis, and slightly longer stays in half-terms and holidays. Therefore the number of days within any one year amounts to a minimum of thirty days, and a possible maximum of forty. It has been customary in the past for boys to spend periods of between two and five years within the scheme. Flexibility in terms of time is seen as an essential factor of the work. As a worker, one can only move as fast as one's clients, and any treatment plan must be based upon the client's ability and potential for movement – this will not be the same in each and every case.

The actual content of the short residential periods is of considerable importance. The quality and nature of this underlines the whole scheme. The concern is to provide a therapeutic experience rather than a training programme, to inculcate self-awareness, self-respect and personal integrity, rather than suppress individuality and impose standards; to nourish, encourage and support rather than to punish; and to promote ego development rather than conformity through external discipline.

This does not mean that there is no structure or no control, but that the emphasis is on remedial rather than corrective measures. The concern is with repairing and enabling rather than punishing. Structure, activities, routine play a part in this, but the development, and the course, of personal relationships is of the essence, both in the one-to-one situations and in groups.

There are three main areas of operation during a weekend, with a delicate balance between them:

The provision of a satisfactory group learning experience;

The provision of the opportunities for satisfactory relationships to develop between staff and boy and a boy and members of his peer group;

The provision of a wide variety of experiences, through which a boy's own horizons may be broadened, through which his own self-confidence may be increased and through which these all-important relationships may be developed.

Boys arrive at Northorpe on Friday evenings and stay until Sunday evening. With 8-10 boys each weekend and approximately 3 adults, it gives a fairly high ratio of adults to boys. An attempt is made throughout the weekend to establish a warm, caring atmosphere, a clearly defined framework within which boys may move. For those accustomed to no controls at all, they will find that, in order to live successfully and happily together during the weekend, certain "standards" should be observed. To those used to a rigid, inflexible environment, freedom to move is what they will find. It is important that we are able to assess when exactly adult intervention is necessary.

Throughout the entire exercise in group living and learning over the weekend, there are many opportunities for one-to-one relationships to develop between peers and between boys and adults. The vehicle to facilitate the development of these relationships may be the activity, the shared experience; this way, conversations are not forced, but develop naturally. For example, when the staff take the youngest boys swimming, they find them to be clinging and dependent initially. But in teaching the boys to swim and dive, several things happen. The boys develop a new skill, increase in self-confidence and, throughout the entire process there is a growing relationship between the worker and the child which can be seen to enhance the boy's own sense of personal worth. And this carries over into other areas.

There are, however, areas left free for the boys to structure themselves. The choice of activity is theirs and, although the staff may feel that an activity is good for a boy and that new experiences are beneficial, they have to fight the tendency to cram the weekends full. Often they find it is far more useful to spend whole days not involved in any structured activity, simply relaxing, talking, listening to the record player, watching the television, or playing games, with people moving in their own time and their own way from one area to another.

One of the essential ingredients of the treatment process is the linking of the treatment to the child's home life. This is of utmost importance in the treatment of children, whether or not they are in residential care. If indeed the aims of treatment are curative and preventive, it is the forging of this link between the child's treatment and his home life which gives the treatment efficiency and effectiveness. Whilst the child is involved in the scheme, staff from Northorpe are visiting him and his family regularly at home, so that the residential periods are not isolated, unconnected experiences, but part of a continuum, an integrated treatment plan.

The advantage to the child is considerable when the same people who care for him, accept him as he is, also control, encourage and attend to him, and enter with him into close meaningful relationships whilst he is in this short-term care. These are the same people who visit him at home, befriend the family, help him to make use of his residential experience within his home environment, to learn and develop from it and apply it and make it relevant in his day-to-day living. For the staff at Northorpe, the opportunity to translate and synchronise the work in one setting with that in another is an enormous benefit. By spending whole weekends living with the boys, they know so much more about them, are able to make deeper and more effective relationships and are presented with an unequalled opportunity for carrying out effective treatment and casework in the homes.

Nottinghamshire Social Services

Nottinghamshire Social Services Department began experimenting with intermediate treatment fairly early and at one time were running eleven or twelve groups simultaneously, involving perhaps 100 children. These groups were based on an earlier experimental project which developed several different styles of work. Social workers in the department conceived of intermediate treatment as essentially a social work activity, although other professionals such as teachers and youth workers could be taught the skills and knowledge necessary for working with small groups of deprived adolescents.

The first type of work involved residential periods away from the local community. Groups had a series of evenly spaced weekends camping, or in youth hostel-type accommodation, beginning, however, with a block week in order to establish group identity. The total number of days spent away met the 1969 Act's 30 day requirement, though additional sessions were conducted occasionally in order to plan and discuss the trips. The longer period at the outset of a group's life was designed to enable it to become more established, and more conscious of a group identity, than would have been the case were its members meeting only for weekends throughout the year. The need was for a fairly long and intensive initial group experience. The practice also developed of ending groups with a similarly long period, in order that the group's termination could be marked appropriately – rather than have it tapering off with just another weekend.

All the groups are small, usually no more than nine young people, and with a high staff-child ratio, at least two, and usually three, staff members being involved. The initial experiment included children whose ages ranged between 12 and 15, while careful selection excluded the very disturbed and those totally unwilling to participate. Most of the groups are mixed, though occasionally all boys groups have been set up.

Activities during weekend and block week sessions include walking and climbing, field and table games, visits to beaches, swimming pools, ice rinks, cinemas, museums, railways and castles. These activities are planned and discussed at length with the children concerned, and structured in order to develop their self-esteem, avoiding, as far as possible, any experience which might be construed by the child as another personal failure.

Great stress is laid on informality in relation between staff and children, even when this situation leads, as it usually does, to testing out, and the expression of negative and hostile feelings. Such expression not only provides material for discussion and mutual learnings, but brings about a degree of laterality in relationships between supervisor and supervised which is impossible in the normal casework setting.

The relation between intermediate treatment and supervision was, indeed, one of the issues to which attention in the initial experiment was devoted. Of four original groups, two comprised three staff members working with children from their own caseloads, and two involved staff working with children from other social workers' caseloads. When the groups had become established, the children's attitudes towards their supervisors and groupworkers were sought. The results were illuminating. With few exceptions, the children identified with the groupworkers, whether the latter were their supervisors or not, to the extent, in one or two cases, of believing that the group workers were their supervisors, even when this was not the case. In this situation, the relationship with the supervisor compared unfavourably with the relationship with the group worker, and there was little evidence to suggest that good relationships formed in the group setting were transferred back to the casework situation. In contrast, relationships with supervisors who were included in the same groups as their own cases tended to improve considerably. The absence of transfer from the group setting to other situations, however, could still be observed in that relationships with other authority figures such as teachers may have deteriorated.

A pattern of developing responsibility is encouraged in the groups, and an attempt has been made to describe in outline a programme model. Certain aspects of relationship and task performance can be developed over successive weekends, with the accent always on gradually passing over responsibility for the running the groups to all their members and not just the social workers. Thus, while the introductory five days may see the establishment of roles, horizontal relationships and a basis for activity and discussion, over successive weekends the planning and organisation of various tasks — from the mundane necessities such as cooking and washing up to the trickier issues of behaviour control and future activities — become the responsibility of the group as a whole. Each stage requires lengthy discussion, and groups obviously respond differently, at times regressing and becoming disorganised. This is a very vulnerable situation for the social workers, who must not lose their nerve, be prepared always to negotiate, and be willing to share their anxieties.

A second pattern of work was established when a group of sixteen boys formed a more community-based group meeting once every week during an evening. This "club" was run by a social worker (who was also the supervisor of most of the boys involved) aided by volunteers. The club had a turn-over of membership as some of the boys dropped out after leaving school and starting work, and were replaced by others on supervision or at risk. Activities in this group closely resemble the normal youth club, with some community service activities included — digging gardens for the elderly, decorating, chopping wood. There has also been some socio-drama which proved a useful medium of expression. Like the other groups, young people involved in this club tend to avoid formal discussion situations, preferring off-hand, though still significant, discussion in informal settings, for example in the car or mini-bus.

The results of this second type of group were particularly encouraging. Twelve months before, these sixteen boys had been responsible for a total of 300 offences, but, within a year of the group's existence, only one of them was reported for further offences.

The beginnings of parallel work with parents' groups also emerged in the Nottinghamshire project when two fathers of delinquent boys formed the nucleus of a group meeting with community workers and social workers in order to obtain premises for a youth club. Premises were eventually found, and are now used not only by this club, but also by a variety of consumer groups including the elderly and handicapped. This club is an open club, run by the fathers of delinquent boys with volunteer and social work assistance. The effect has been further to dissolve the professional-client form of relationship between parents and social workers, who are now seen not as remote authority figures, but as concerned and involved people who acknowledge that problem-solving is a reciprocal and not a one-sided process.

Pontefract Handicraft Club and Activity Centre

This facility has developed since the early 1960s, out of the awareness of a Pontefract probation officer who perceived the need to develop an alternative setting to the office for work with boys in the 10-16 age group.

The club was intended as a setting where such boys might have the opportunity to develop 'meaningful relationships with adults and peers in an independent and secure atmosphere where they can get satisfaction from socially accepted challenges'.[2] Over the years, a group of local people provided financial, practical and professional support, and the Quakers were primarily involved in the slow development of the present club premises on land belonging to the Society of Friends in Pontefract.

Originally, activities occupied the adjacent Friends' Meeting House. Later a prefabricated building was used. Currently, the solid, unbeautiful, but entirely functional, two-storey premises comprise workshops and a toolroom for woodwork, art and music, a judo room and games room, a refreshment bar and canteen area, garaging, and canoe and equipment storage, as well as other rooms. Internally the premises were conceived as capable of continual adaptation to meet changing needs, and the involvement of boys in this work was seen as an important aspect of the work of the club.

The club is situated on the south side of the main Wakefield to Goole road through Pontefract, adjacent to multi-storey flats a few yards to the north, and extensive council estates to the south. Most of the membership has been drawn from this latter area. Additionally, a wider catchment area has been drawn upon, through referrals by social services departments, child guidance clinics, schools and the probation service.

A key aspect of policy has been the focusing upon work in a small group setting with 'the inadequate basic membership'. With the activities and level of acceptable behaviour geared to this group, it was found useful to allow them each to bring along a mate if they wished. A further third of the club membership consisted of a heterogeneous group, many of whom referred themselves.

The supply of staff and resources to the club has been maintained over the years by strenuous local efforts. Close links have been forged with local education, youth and social services departments, who have supplied instructors, activity leaders and financial grants.

Within the past four years, Dr. Barnardo's have been invited to help the project, and have become progressively more involved. In January 1974, Barnardo's took on the overall responsibility for the management of the club, in the context of its ongoing links with statutory agencies, and currently Barnardo's provide four full-time members of staff, including the project director, assistant leader, outdoor pursuits leader and social worker.

The club is open three evenings a week from 6.30 to 9.00 p.m., and the nature of many activities – especially outdoor pursuits – is such that, particularly during school holidays, they tend to spill over into the day time and other periods when staff are available. Additional to the three instructors provided by the education authority for evening sessions, there are three activity leaders from the youth service, and a number of ancillary workers and local volunteers.

Since 1971, the club has made increasing use of outdoor pursuits facilities at Semerwater, in Wensleydale. Activities are structured, selective and staff-intensive, though within the overall framework each Semerwater course takes on its own individual character. Each course comprises about eight boys and four leaders and extends over a period of about two months. Evenings in the club doing preparatory work, the four weekends away, and subsequent discussion and review form an organic whole.

In the past, courses have fallen into three broad groups: those for boys at risk; for those on probation needing greater involvement; for those who have failed on probation, as an alternative to longer institutional experience. Courses involve club staff and a number of volunteers, mainly from professions closely related to social work. On various occasions, a social worker or probation officer has joined a course, either for the four weekends in entirety, or for shorter pre-arranged visits to his clients. In this way, the club and Semerwater have provided both an added dimension to casework, and an independent resource in its own right for client benefit.

Administrative support and supervisory services are provided currently through Barnardo's Yorkshire Divisional Office at Horsforth, Leeds. A locally based advisory panel meets regularly, and worked as the club's management committee until January 1974. The constitution of the new body is not yet finalised, but its task for the interim period are seen as: acting as liaison between the project and the local community; giving advice on current policy, planning and development; giving support to club staff; acting as a fund-raising resource. Membership of the panel includes magistrates, divisional officers from agencies supplying staff and resources, Quakers and other interested people under the chairmanship of a local headmaster. Barnardo's staff, including the project director, attend meetings.

Currently, project staff are working to clarify the club's policy in terms of developments since Martin Rowntree made the statement of its aims and methods (already referred to) in March 1971. This review should lead to the formulation of a development plan by Autumn 1974.

Five orders containing intermediate treatment requirements have been made in local courts in April and May 1974. All five boys are club attenders, and discussions are in progress with probation and social service departments (who are responsible for two and three of the boys, respectively) to establish formal channels of referral and review. The question of the role of the project staff vis-a-vis the involvement of statutory supervising agencies is under discussion. Barnardo's social workers already operate a Family Care Service in the Pontefract area, so the boundaries between such work and the work of local statutory agencies are already subject to regular review. Task definition in this area needs attention in the context of the overall orientation of the project, which is seen by the director in terms of taking individual referrals in a family and neighbourhood setting, and taking into account agency-client interaction, rather than restricting task boundaries of the project to a clinical concentration on assessing and treating the individual needs of the child.

Youth Development Trust Project, Wythenshawe, Manchester

This project is operated within the context of one of four action-research projects which together comprise the work of the Youth Development Trust. The Trust raises its funds for the projects from a variety of sources, each project receiving money from a source appropriate to the specific nature of its work. In the case of the intermediate treatment project, funding both for the research component and the fieldwork is entirely from Manchester Social Services, through two annual grants, one to the Y.D.T. and one to Manchester University, which employs the research worker, though with an agreed responsibility to Y.D.T. The Department also provides a building, rent, heating and lighting included. They provide board and lodgings for the project's Community Service Volunteer, and they pay directly for the residential sessions (1963 Act money) separate from the grant to Y.D.T. The Intermediate Treatment Project, like the others, has a commitment to produce a written evaluation of its work at the end of its period of activity.

The two original appointments, a project leader (fieldwork) and the research worker were of equal status, though employed by different bodies. These two performed the necessary groundwork before the appointment of a second member of fieldwork staff and the C.S.W. The first phase of group work began in November 1972, and between that time and June 1973, four groups were completed. Working with these groups in the context of the legislation raised a number of questions and issues about intermediate treatment and about the ways in which the staff were working, but which could not be resolved while the work was actively going ahead. The group work was therefore stopped for a period in order that time could be spent in making some evaluation of the work and the way in which it was being tackled. The project leader came to the conclusion that the issues raised could never be resolved within the framework of intermediate treatment as defined by the Act, and resigned from the project.

In September 1973, the second fieldworker was promoted to project leader, and together with the research worker she drew up a set of proposals for a second phase of work which took into account a'l the difficulties of the first phase and suggested ways of reducing them. Phase 2 has been in operation since November 1973, and will be completed in mid-summer, 1974, when the staff will again look at its work and decide upon the next course of action on the basis of a comparison between the two phases.

The project is essentially community-based. The staff accept the philosophy of intermediate treatment which strives to make it a positive experience which will expand the cultural horizons of the referrals. They interpret this to mean an experience which is within their reach, and not one in which the environment in further deprivation. For this reason, the project is based in the environment in which the children live, and it uses resources which are accessible to them whether or not they attend the group. This applies also to places to which the groups go for the residential period of the treatment.

By operating a facility which is group-work based, the aim is to help the children acquire a greater sense of responsibility for themselves, their behaviour their activities; by helping them towards increasing self-confidence, it is hoped that they will gain in maturity and acquire a better level of communication with adults, particularly those in authority. The area of relationships is a central concern, and this is worked at through the group work method by using the relationships within the groups between members, child and child, adult and adult, adult and child, and between sub-groups within the group. Using the relationships within the group, it is possible to help members to become more self-aware, both in and out of the group situation, and to help them to relate what they learn in the group to their lives outside it.

Although group work orientated, the project recognises the need for work with individuals, and by providing a number of adults in a group, the members are given a choice of relationships and can select according to their needs. The project is committed to action-research through membership of the Y.D.T., and is not only geared to an ongoing evaluation of its work and to changing it as appropriate, but also accepts a need to test out different kinds of groups with different structure, memberships and adult composition.

In *Phase 1,* referrals came from Probation, Social Services, Child Guidance and, on rare occasions, from schools. All referrals were in the 11-14 age range, and a group was never bigger than 10 in number, plus 3 staff members. Mostly the groups were all male, and if girls were referred, a group never contained less than two. Each group met twice weekly, immediately after school, for 2½ hour sessions over a period of 3 months, and in addition, the fieldwork staff met with a consultant once a week for 1½ hours. After every group session, the staff had a meeting the following morning for about 2 hours, and tried to create a staff-group perception of the session. One staff member would write up the record after the meeting. Staff members visited parents of participants, their supervising officers and the schools, keeping them up to date and exchanging information. This happened about once a fortnight, in the hope that these 'significant others' would be enabled to change their perceptions of the child and relate to him in a different way. The groups had the specific task of "working at relationships". Midway through a group's life, it went on a residential session in an isolated place in the country where it could be exposed to an intensive group experience.

This structure threw up a great many problems. Sometimes a situation was created which was directly contrary to the project's aims. The experience was often a depriving one, and it was felt that this was partly due to the short time-span and the intensity of twice-weekly meetings. There was frequently a hierarchical structure in the groups, maintained by bullying, which said something about the way the staff group was operating. The task was not always accepted, and a group with a strong sub-culture was capable of avoiding real communication with the staff. Often the task was too abstract a concept for the members to understand.

The method of record-keeping seemed to absorb a disproportionate amount of staff-time. Relationships with parents and other agencies were necessarily superficial in the short time-span and achieved little beyond the exchange of information. Also very gradually the relationship with supervisors deteriorated because there were obvious gains for the children, but once the group ended the supervisors found it very difficult to pick up where the project left off, as they had not been part of the experience and some children regressed very quickly after the group ended. Clearly the situation was an unhelpful one, both to the client and supervisor. The groups were set up in such a way that they were isolated from the reasons for their existence. Members had a hazy understanding of the project's relationship to the referring agency. They did not have any clear understanding of why they were in the group, how they had been selected, or what the group had to do with anything they had done.

Phase 2 tried to come to grips with these problems:

The time span is extended from 3 months to 6 months, on a once-weekly basis for a 3 hour session immediately after school.

The group membership is selected from each of only 2 caseloads, and the supervisor becomes a group member also, in a capacity as staff. The age-range is either 11-14 or 14-16, with a maximum of ten members, and if any girls, a minimum of 3. If a group has siblings, it has been found preferable to include more than one pair.

The project staff have separate areas of responsibility in relating to different agencies, and each has a responsibility for specific groups. They act as floating members of other groups and are therefore available if need be.

The consultancy session is open to all staff who work in the groups with the project staff — social workers, probation officers, education welfare officers, teachers — and is an opportunity for all these agencies to work together in intermediate treatment. It is in this way meeting one of the other aims of the project, in providing a neutral setting in which agencies with different approaches can discuss their work, their perspectives, and can come to understand each other better.

Record keeping is the responsibility of the staff-member who is employed in the project. The records serve to communicate to other project staff, the consultant and other staff members of that particular group not only a record of the session, but also the perceptions of the record-keeper, which are then the basis for discussion at group-staff meetings, which take place on average once a month. Project staff meet once a fortnight: group staff meet once a month.

Parallel parents' groups are set up with the groups which meet once a month. This is based on a policy that as supervisors are involved in the group work, there is no need for project staff to visit homes except when it is something that directly concerns the project. So the parents are encouraged to become involved in the project rather than vice-versa.

The groups are set a specific task, as an aid to the primary task of "working at relationships" — for example, making a film, or organising a camp. The residential session is planned with an awareness that the experience should be one which the members can repeat in some way once they have left the group, if they so wish.

Continuity — the problem that when the group ends the members are even more deprived — is tackled on two levels. Firstly, the inclusion of the supervising officer as a member of the group means that the relationship is deepended, strengthened, and continues after the group ends. If the officer can arrange it, it may also be possible to continue some form of group supervision with his half of the group. Secondly, the project provides an open session when members of any groups, past or present, may attend. The open session is not a group — it is a time when project staff have committed themselves to be at the Centre, and when members may come to use the facilities, meet other members, and otherwise maintain some of the relationships they have established. In this way the members can wean themselves away as and when they feel they are ready.

Note

Details of sources for these descriptions and, where appropriate, names of contributors, will be found in the Appendix. The analysis that follows in Chapter 4 is based, in all cases, on material more extensive than that included here, which is necessarily limited for reasons of space.

4 TEN PROJECTS: AN ANALYSIS

Having rejected the regional schemes and the "official" view of intermediate treatment, it is our intention in the second half of this book to develop a "theory" of intermediate treatment which is, to a greater extent, based on the experience of projects such as those described in the previous chapter, though we shall attempt to unify that experience and go beyond it. To begin with, we shall look at those projects in greater detail, focus on some of the more important issues they raise, and draw attention to some of the differences and similarities which they exhibit.

It is obvious that the projects do not put intermediate treatment into practice in exactly the same way, so let us first consider some of the factors that determine their various styles of work. There appear to be five important ones.

a) Perceived problems and needs.

Not all delinquents have the same problem, even if they often respond to their situations in similar ways and make similar associations. The causes of delinquency range over a great number of factors. If one of the objectives of treatment (or of prevention) in general, and of intermediate treatment in particular, is to come to grips, even in a marginal way, with these factors, then some of the groups, one might expect, will be predicted in the problems of their members. This is obviously true of the Islington centre, a provision for truants. It is also true of some of the groups in the Albany scheme which consisted of boys from single-parent families. In both these cases, some attempt is made to make the nature of the group work relevant to the problem in question. The original objective of the Islington centre was reintegration into the school, the group being set up on a more or less free school basis, while at the Albany, the boys were given the opportunity to discuss and work through the problems they faced as members of effectively fatherless families. Another example is the Eastern Ravens project, one of whose objectives is to help young people understand and perhaps overcome the limitations of a deprived environment.

b) Referral procedure.

Patterns of referral have varied and will vary from agency to agency and authority to authority. Some authorities have already made arrangements for the combining of funds available under the 1969 Act with those available under the 1963 Act, thus by-passing two key financial conditions of the 1969 Act: (i) that a court appearance is necessary; (ii) that the facility used should appear in the regional plans. In such instances, a much more flexible referral procedure can be used as the child has no need to appear before the court (whether or not he has actually committed an offence). Thus, intermediate treatment could take place on a community basis (like Eastern Ravens, or the National Children's Bureau intermediate treatment projects) or on a club basis, catering for self-referrals and friends in addition to social work referrals (Haylands, Pontefract, Higher Clarence). In other cases, however, where 1969 Act money may be less accessible, referrals will come from the courts in ones and twos, and it may be more difficult to work on such a basis. In these cases, a pattern of referral to specific groups is more likely, even if the group uses community based facilities. These groups are specifically for referred children, rather than having a "turn-over" basis, as the club-type projects have, and may have specific termination points as well. Examples of this pattern are the two residential centres, Northorpe Hall and Dallington Lodge, together with Wythenshawe, the Albany, and Nottinghamshire. Prior to the coming into effect of the 1969 Act, none of these projects, of course, were taking children with intermediate treatment requirements. But they were experimenting with the pattern of referrals that would arise from court proceeedings. In Nottinghamshire intermediate treatment was, in any case, conceived as a means of "keeping the children out of trouble" and, if possible, out of care. It was therefore understood as a provision for extremely high risk delinquents who have come before the court on several occasions, so that, aside from experimenting with the possibilities of the Act, the pattern of referrals was bound to be related to court appearances.

c) Resources and setting.

The resources available to different areas will also, of course, vary considerably. Not every authority has access to a Northorpe Hall, for example, or to an Albany. Nor does every deprived area have suitable youth facilities in which activities can be based. Some Nottinghamshire groups have had to meet in area offices, while Eastern Ravens were provided by the county council with toilets which they were able to convert for use as a club room. Where community based facilities are available, it is evidently a good idea to make use of them and develop them, though how far the community can be involved in the intermediate treatment programme depends on other factors. How far other children from the same area can be involved in the programme is related to factors such as resources, manpower and referral procedure. At the other end of the spectrum, it may be that the residential centres have some limitations: neither Northorpe Hall nor Dallington Lodge is the community which it serves, and to this extent community contact may be more limited. However, Northorpe's intensive family casework, and Dallington's community projects help to overcome these limitations. Even so, they may miss the benefits — and problems — of a centre like the Islington project, which is firmly located in the community served. Another factor related to manpower and setting relates to the numbers that can be catered for. Where these are relatively small, at a residential centre, for example, a pattern of referral to specific groups is also likely to emerge.

d) Historical factors.

It is not always easy to transform existing facilities and resources in order to accommodate them to a new style of work. In many cases, therefore, a compromise may have to be worked out between the demands and objectives of intermediate treatment and the history and expectations of the facilities available. An example of this point may be seen in the Albany situation, where community resource had for several years been instrumental in helping local groups to organise interest groups and political action. The agency's commitment was therefore necessarily partisan, identifying closely with local residents. The organiser of the project therefore took it to be essential to play down his social services identity, and sought to remove all elements of compulsion from the scheme. Other factors that can be included under this heading concern the attitudes of people in the community to the facilities being used – in the case of Higher Clarence, for example, the antagonism of uninvolved local people, and of the youth club's management committee, was a factor which at times inhibited the project's activities.

e) Statutory and voluntary.

There may occasionally be differences between projects run by, or closely associated with, statutory agencies and those run by voluntary agencies. For example, while the statutory agencies will be more concerned with their responsibilities towards the courts and to their relations with the police, the voluntary agencies may give more attention to the problems of the environment and communities in which they are located or in which they work, and to the way in which these problems are perceived by their clients. In terms of objectives, this difference can be illustrated by Nottinghamshire's aim of keeping the children out of trouble, and Eastern Ravens' aim of helping them to understand, come to terms with, and perhaps try to change, their environment.

In the context of these variables, it may be useful now to place the projects considered here into broad categories, differentiated in ways suggested by the points outlined above.

(A) Residential (Northorpe Hall, Dallington Lodge)

(B) Specific groups (community-based) (Wythenshawe, Eastern Ravens, the Albany, Nottinghamshire).

(C) Club type (Haylands, Higher Clarence, Pontefract).

(D) Day centre (Islington).

It is not suggested that this list is exhaustive of intermediate treatment styles. It is merely the most economical list of categories into which the projects here considered can be fitted. Even then, some cases are slightly blurred. The Nottinghamshire groups, for example, while they are mainly of the specific referral kind, differ in their use of community facilities.

We may characterise briefly the main differences between these categories though what we have to say will have been implicit in the earlier discussion.

(A) the two residential centres are not, of course, residential in the sense of Section 12.2(a) of the 1969 CYPA (the ninety day provision), but only in the same sense that they are removed from the communities they serve, and the groups stay for brief periods — usually weekends — in the care of the centre staff. Dallington Lodge (and, to a lesser extent, Northorpe Hall) have experimented with other forms of provision: midweek activity groups, playgroups, outdoor challenge activities and a school unit. With limited space and numbers, both centres cater for small, specific groups, and both are able to engage in casework with the children and their families — an extension of the work that is generally not possible in the same way with larger numbers and a "turn-over basis" for membership (unless referring supervisors are actively involved).

(B) Again, the central feature here is the specific group, this time in a more community-based setting. Common to the three projects other than Nottinghamshire are facilities situated within the communities served which can be used as a basis of operations — although trips, camps and weekends away still figure in the various programmes. Nottinghamshire use such facilities where available although, as a social services department, it lacks the secure base in the community which other organisations have. Hence, the groups may not be so deeply rooted in the community setting, and more emphasis may be placed on the periods spent away as a basis for the essential therapeutic work. This factor is supported by the referral procedure described earlier.

(C) the distinguishing feature here is a very flexible referral system, which includes self-referrals and friends in addition to those actually referred from social work agencies. Thus the structure is more like that of a conventional youth club (though with certain differences), with youth club facilities, usually situated in the community served, being used. The implication of this flexible referrals system is clear: larger numbers than is the case with specific groups (although Higher Clarence had two groups which were, to some extent, limited in size), and a club-like "turn-over" of clients, rather than the pattern of definite referrals to a specific group. Pontefract, since being taken over by Barnardo's is thinking along the lines of more intensive work with the actual referrals — the "real clients" — which might move it closer to category (B).

(D) Unlike the three categories outlined so far, the Islington project does not rely on more or less isolated "sessions", but rather seeks to cater for a number of children on a day-care basis at a centre located in the community. Here, of course, perception of a particular problem largely determines the style of work adopted and its medium-term objectives. But this kind of problem is only a special case of a more general one; in the sphere or education, the school embodies features similar to those in society at large, which different children find variously threatening. Its importance lies in the fact that schooling is a statutory requirement on the child and, this being the case, non-attendance is itself a problem, besides being a symptom of other problems. Thus, attempts to cope with this problem are not structurally dissimilar from the other, more general, projects we discuss: experience is presented in a non-threatening group framework, and the centre acts as a buffer between the truant and the full force of the law that could be brought down upon him. In the nature of the case, the referral procedure is specific, though it has been a source of some concern that such centres cannot cater for more children. To do so, however, might undermine the therapeutic intent: education on a small, and more personalised, scale.

Aims

A common theme runs through the projects' various statements of their aims: the importance of relationships – between child and child as well as child and adult. This is, in itself, enough to cast doubt on the supposition, if it still holds currency, that the essential point of intermediate treatment will be the provision of activities of a healthy, or improving, nature. This is not to say, of course, that the projects eschew activities altogether On the contrary, in most cases, activities of one kind or another are considered a necessary focus for the group work. It is rather that the activity is regarded more as a vehicle for work on relationships than as something from which developing relationships are a mere spin-off.

As one might expect, the projects working with small specific groups can afford to be the most ambitious about their work with relationships. For the larger groups, run on a club-tyoe basis (Haylands, Pontefract, Higher Clarence), the works seems to be conceived more as a holding operation, a supportive measure, rather than as direct intervention; and the need to bring interest and greater stimulation into the children's lives receives proportionately greater stress in their reports. Even in those cases, however, it is a primary aim to provide an opportunity for the children to develop close, consistent and meaningful relationships with adults and peers.

There are, perhaps, three relationships we can consider: the child's relationship with adults, as representatives of the social world from which he might feel alienated, and as authority figures; the child's relationship with his peers, which forms a part of the supportive framework of his delinquency; and, finally, the child's relationship with himself, his self-image, self-esteem. Let us consider these in reverse order.

Self-confidence, self-awareness, self-esteem: here are three related qualities which nearly all the projects explicitly seek to encourage. Self-confidence and self-esteem need little comment in the light of the discussion of the first chapter. The delinquent's failed identity, and his association with others in a similar position (or his rejection of all associations) is one of the main supports of his behaviour. His self-esteem, diminished in most socially acceptable fields, can be rebuilt only in socially unacceptable activity. His confidence in the situations into which society would thrust him wanes, and is replaced by anxiety or bravado: in the educational context, it can result in truancy if the force of delinquent association within the school is not great enough to overcome this lack of self-confidence. These remarks also suggest why several projects refer to the need to develop the child's ability to make decisions. This has two aspects: firstly, the need to develop his confidence and self-awareness to the extent that he can better cope with the world as he finds it, and pick out his own path through it, conscious of himself as a person with certain desires and needs (something he may hitherto have only been able to do on the margins of society); secondly, the need to offer an opportunity for structured experiences that he himself has helped to determine – a change from his former, and usual, status as a subject of a vicarious, and apparently arbitrary, decision-making process. Hence, the insistence of Wythenshawe and Nottinghamshire on democratic group structures. At the tactical level, as previous chapters suggested, transferring responsibility for decision making to the group's members also helps to overcome the "neutralising" tendencies of the delinquent, who is able to use that former status to justify his distrust of, and hostility towards, the forces and agencies which govern his life. Self-awareness completes this picture in a general way: the child's developing awareness of himself as a potentially self-determining person, trying to combat a deprived and damaging environment.

It is the point at which relationships between child and child, and child and adult, become the focus of concern that certain problems and anxieties begin to emerge. Delinquent associations are not only a supportive framework for delinquent activity and attitudes, they are also subject to those attitudes, and hence there arises a problem of behaviour in the group as well as a problem of coping with the norms which it supports in relation to the outside world. The first of these problems is, of course, magnified with regard to the adult figures. Though it does not always emerge explicitly in the reports, is is yet another point of the small group framework; for if a sense of group identity can be encouraged, and the sense of commitment and belonging that go with it, the problems of intra group relationships are thereby lessened, and a foundation will have been laid for developing non-delinquent attitudes and relationships. This is, at any rate, an objective, though how it is worked out is another matter. The problems associated with it will also be discussed under the heading "authority and control". As an objective, it cannot finally be disentangled from those relating to the child's relationship with himself. For example, if one is to encourage "verbalisation rather than acting out" (Albany), this is in itself an exercise in self-awareness; equally, developing self-confidence in the context of the group experience is part and parcel of improving relationships between individuals based on mutual and self-respect.

Even more problematic are relationships between child and adult, especially if the adult is conceived as an authority figure. Some of the projects seen to exhibit signs of uneasiness in considering this point. In a low-key way, it is possible to talk simply of the adults providing "close and consistent relationships" and creating an "atmosphere of trust" (Higher Clarence), while, at the other end of the spectrum, we find something slightly more ambitious: " . . . help them communicate better with adults and give them an understanding of the nature of authority" (Wythenshawe). What *is* the nature of authority? And how is the child supposed to understand it? Is it something he must learn to accept when others claim it, or something he must be allowed to challenge and explore? Most of the projects implicitly take the first view. Dallington Lodge, for example, states that one of their aims is to "provide a chance to make choices and challenge norms". Two comments may be appropriate here. First, the answer to the original question is that, in practice, authority is both, and it is up to the individual as to where he is prepared to draw the line (so that, in intermediate treatment, this objective again cannot be separated out from the individual developments in the child, his self-awareness and evolving perceptions). Second, all the projects are committed to authority *within* the group as being something achieved by personal qualities, something predicated on the relationships an adult can develop with the children, rather than something imposed by virtue of adulthood, or a position as a project staff-number. Generalised, of course, this commitment has considerable implications for social work and education (Islington talk of "removing responsibility on to the group experience rather than allowing it to depend on the authority of the teacher, quo teacher"). Meanwhile, the first comment suggests that a realistic objective would be to exhibit to the children the kind of compromise we all make in regard to authority — the points at which we challenge it, the points at which we accept it — in order that they can make their own decisions. Only, and this is an important rider, we must be prepared to find that the points at which they are prepared to challenge and accept may be different from ours.

Longer term objectives some times express the effects which, it is hoped, work along these lines will have, especially in the case of the more community based projects which, perhaps, more than the residential and social services projects, are directly conscious of the children's situation within the community. Both the Albany and the Hayland's project reports talk of putting the children in touch with ordinary youth service facilities (though Haylands have experienced difficulties in achieving this aim). But the same concern, that of gradually phasing the children back into socially acceptable forms of association is encountered in the other projects. At its most general, of course, it is simply the aim of enabling the children to "live well adjusted law-abiding lives in their own families" (Northorpe Hall) or of "keeping them out of trouble" (Nottinghamshire). In the educational setting, it is expressed in Islington's long term hope of re-integration, although, in this case, the very concreteness of the objective serves to highlight the difficulties and dangers associated with it (after their unsuccessful attempt, Islington conceived of a "half-way house" between the centre and the school, though located within the latter). The longer term objectives should, however, be taken in the context of those already discussed: the development of relationships and attitudes in the children. It should not be imagined that intermediate treatment is simply a more effective way of stopping delinquency and nothing more. It is rather an attempt to come to grips with some of delinquency's causes, as we have seen; and in this context, improved behaviour, and fewer convictions, are a welcome consequence rather than an immediate aim.

While other agencies, especially the courts and the police, will look to the standards of improved behaviour and fewer court appearances as a measure of intermediate treatment's success, the previous paragraph suggests that, for the actual practitioner, this may not be the only, and perhaps not the first, concern, although this may be more true of the voluntary agencies than of the statutory ones. It also suggests that there may be cases in which, on the contrary, there are divergences between the two sets of criteria — the visible, concrete evidence of reconviction rates and the more subtle evidence, perceptible only to the practitioner, perhaps, of changes in the child's attitudes and relationships — divergences which may well result in occasional crises of conscience (a phenomenon not unknown to other youth workers). For the social worker, such crises will be particularly acute, raising once again, in a particular form, the perennial question of the social worker's role in society: cosmetician or politician? Increasingly, perhaps, the same dilemma will become apparent in the educational field. Are the example of Islington and the free schools, for instance, in the long term designed as therapeutic — matching Islington's original aim of reintegration — or as "catalysts for change", as in the case of another day-care centre, modelled on Islington, which has recently been set up in Haringey?

We may note here yet another complication for the statutory agencies and the voluntary organisations directly linked with them (Nottinghamshire, Wythenshawe, Northorpe Hall, Dallington Lodge, the Albany). This is the question of the relation of intermediate treatment to supervision. Both Nottinghamshire and Wythenshawe set out to operate intermediate treatment as "an aid to supervision" (one of the themes of official literature) or as "intensive supervision". For historical reasons, explained above, this was an element deliberately played down by the Albany project. The cases of Northorpe Hall and Dallington Lodge are interesting in that these independent agencies actually take over the casework from the social work services. The point here, however, is what form, in the long term, this relation will take. Is it simply an "aid" to supervision, as Wythenshawe suggest? Or is the relation reversed, as the practice of Northorpe Hall and Dallington Lodge begin to imply? Or, to go even further, does intermediate treatment become a model for a different *form* of supervision, as other passages from the Wythenshawe report suggest, and as the concept of "intensive supervision" (Nottinghamshire) may be intended? Is intermediate treatment, in the form these projects give it, a model for a new kind of social work relationship?

In closing this section, it hardly needs to be added that the projects do see themselves as positive alternatives to care, though this emerges, in their reports, most explicitly in the case of the residential and specific group categories — not surprisingly since, as was suggested earlier, these projects receive nearly all their referrals from the courts (or will increasingly do so) and, as small groups, can work on the problems more intensively than the club-type projects with their membership turn-over and self-referrals. The latter tend to think rather more in preventive terms, though even for them, avoidance of care is an objective only just over the horizon. In this distinction between the specific group and the preventive and community-based project, we can see, perhaps, the beginnings of a two-pronged attack on delinquency and the courts' reactions to it, an attack already outlined in previous chapters. First, the provision, in the community, of richer resources — in terms of facilities and manpower — which, like Eastern Ravens, derive their objectives from the deprivations of the environment in which they are situated (we might also refer again to the National Children's Bureau projects in this respect). Second, for the children who will, inevitably, still come before the court, intermediate treatment will form a buffer possibility between them and care orders, the pattern here being referral, on the basis of an intermediate treatment requirement, into a specific group.

Time Factors

We come now to look at the frequency and duration of groups in the various projects, bearing in mind that the 1969 Act provides for sessions amounting to an aggregate of thirty days in any one year. Three of the projects (Wythenshawe, Nottinghamshire and Dallington Lodge) have geared their programmes specifically to the legislation — Wythenshawe, indeed, being set up to experiment within the framework of the Act. In other cases, however, the legislation has been only a marginal consideration in terms of time factors. We may again note the difference between the specific groups and the club-type projects with their turn-over membership basis. For while the former can be structured to meet the conditions of the Act, the latter work on a much more flexible basis, and there may be no guarantee that any individual child will have a set number of sessions.

If one is going to attempt to meet the conditions of the Act in this respect (and not all the projects seem convinced that this is a good idea), the question arises as to how the thirty days are to be apportioned. Even this question divides into two: whether or not the thirty days will, in fact, be spread over a year, or whether they will be restricted to a more limited, and perhaps more intensive, period.

Two of the projects (Northorpe Hall and Nottinghamshire) do spread the thirty days over the full year, though in the former case there is a possible maximum of forty days, rather than thirty (which is more of a minimum). The difference between them is that whereas Northorpe Hall takes groups for about ten weekends in each year (one every four weeks), Nottinghamshire tends to go slightly longer between weekend sessions, the difference being made up by longer sessions of five or six days away at the beginning and end of the group's duration. It is felt in Nottinghamshire that the longer sessions are useful – at the beginning in order to establish the group's identity, and at the end in order to provide a suitable "rounding off" of the group's life. (Islington also comment on the identity achieved as a result of residential periods away). Both projects prefer a fairly long-term overall involvement. Nottinghamshire talk of an ideal period being perhaps of two years, while Northorpe Hall handles boys for periods ranging from two to five years: "flexibility is essential – one can only move as fast as the client".

Dallington Lodge, modelled, in some respects, on Northorpe Hall, varies the spread between nine months and a year, but, like Nottinghamshire, includes longer sessions of up to a week. In their view, the length of time between sessions that this pattern involves, approximately six weeks, is the longest one can go without losing the cohesion of the group and its importance for the children. It may be that even this period, were it not for the longer sessions at the beginning of the group's life, would be too long.

Wythenshawe, of the projects working with specific groups, are the most intensive though less so now than during the first year when groups met twice a week for a period of three months only. In the second year, however, the project has moved over to a pattern of weekly sessions for a period of six months (with additional camping weeks and weekends). One of the main reasons for this transition was that three months was short enough a period to cause the group members anxiety about its end almost as soon as it had begun, thus making the groups very difficult to bring to a close.

This raises a more general question of whether final dates can, or should, be set at all, over and above the question as to how far off such dates should be. As we have seen, Northorpe Hall is very flexible about this, and Nottinghamshire reasonably so. The club-type projects have less of a problem here as the club opens regularly (once a week, say) and, with a turn-over in membership, is available whenever and for as long as the individual children need it. On the other hand, Dallington Lodge consider that a time limit is necessary "if any consolidation of results is to be aimed at or achieved". In this project, particular groups end at particular times – although the system is flexible enough to allow individuals to continue in new groups. Up to a point, the difference here is one of setting and framework: a project that works with small, specific groups of children referred from social work agencies can, perhaps, think in terms of definite "results" and group achievements. This is less clearly the case in a more open setting, with larger numbers and self referrals in addition to social work referrals. Here, results and achievements are more individualised and, for this reason, it is harder to put definite limits on involvement.

The three club-type projects, as we have seen, follow the pattern of regular opening nights (once a week in the case of Haylands, High Clarence; four or five times a week at Pontefract), and also have occasional outings, weekends or weeks. In these additions, an interesting new possibility emerges, to which Pontefract are currently giving some thought: a kind of combination of the two elements of intermediate treatment in the same project. The club would continue to work as a community-based preventive project, but would also try to work more intensively with the "real" clients – the social work referrals – in trips and camps. However, there might be a danger here of imposing strain on relations between the social work referrals and the others – resentments and jealousies – strain which is, apparently, visible already.

The Albany groups began with a similar basis to that of Wythenshawe, with a three months duration for the group. Like Wythenshawe, however, this pattern only provoked anxieties. Instead of merely lengthening the period of the groups, however, the Albany project opted for an indefinite period of involvement, with this period ranging, in practice, between 2 and 18 months. This, of course, does not reflect the Dallington Lodge philosophy of definite termination points for definite results; but differences of framework and setting must be borne in mind: Dallington Lodge is residential and works in close co-operation with the supervising agency, while the Albany projects are more community based and try to play down the relation with social services. In the case of the latter's school groups, the school provides an established setting in which the children are already placed and in which the groups come together. Given this established setting, whether in the school, or more generally in the community, to fix dates of termination may be rather artificial. (Similarly, of course, the Islington project, working with children who have educational problems, cannot afford to set deadlines for the period of involvement).

Finally, Eastern Ravens work in a very long term framework – groups lasting for up to five or six years (here again the long term provision is associated with a definite community orientation). Currently, however, the project is also devising a scheme which is more closely geared to the requirements of the Act. This new scheme resembles Wythenshawe's current practice; groups will meet for 26 consecutive weeks, with three weekend events near the beginning, middle and end of the scheme. It will be interesting to see how the new scheme fits into the established structure of the project, given the continuation of existing groups, and how the referral and community elements of the project will be combined.

Another issue is the actual length of time spent per session. The Act stipulates that a "day" may refer to any part of a day spent on intermediate treatment, so that the 30-day requirement could be met, at one extreme, by 30 sessions of, say, an hour each, or at the other extreme, by 30 full days (at a residential centre, for example). The two residential projects, of course, do work roughly on a day basis, as do the Nottinghamshire groups, which emphasise periods spent away. The other projects work in sessions lasting anywhere between half an hour (the Albany school group) to three hours (Wythenshawe), with various trips and camping weekends thrown in.

It is evident that (i) "30 days" is a meaningless and arbitrary figure; (ii) that there is a place for programmes of varying intensity, according to the children's needs. Once "30 days" is dropped as a condition of treatment that must be met, the way is open to recognising the difference between weekly half hour sessions and residential weeks, and to integrating them in an overall, coherent, plan of treatment.

Groups and staffing

Again we distinguish between club-type projects and those working with specific groups. The former, of course, work with slightly numbers, though maintain an adult/child ratio almost as high as the other projects. Pontefract handle as many as 40 boys on any one evening and have at their disposal two full time leaders, nine instructors and, in addition, volunteers. Haylands have about 25 boys, averaging roughly 16 a night, and also involve social workers in the staffing. Higher Clarence had rather fewer members in each of its two groups, which covered two different age ranges. Like the other two projects in this category, there was a turn-over of membership, amounting to 50% over 20 months. There was also a turn-over in staff, particularly students, though two leaders, one in each group, remained throughout, while the actual adult-child ratio never exceeded 1:4. The project staff comment that a permanent membership of two adults in each group would, perhaps, have been preferable. This matches the experience of other projects.

The projects operating with specific groups generally have no more than 12 members in each group, and preferably not more than nine or ten. The number of adults is at least two, and usually three. Some of these projects also maintain a limited span of ages (three years in the case of Eastern Ravens and Dallington Lodge). Wythenshawe also point out that the age range should not be too wide, and add that if the groups are to be mixed, they should include at least three girls. This project and Dallington Lodge are also concerned with the importance of "balance" within the group if objectives are to be achieved – a balance in terms of type of child and problems faced. Wythenshawe specify that the referrals for any one group should not come from more than two caseloads, according to their concept of intermediate treatment as an aid to supervision. Like other projects (Albany, Haylands, Higher Clarence, Pontefract and Nottinghamshire) seek to involve social workers in the groups, but go further than the others in laying down a condition: the supervisor must be prepared to participate before his cases are accepted.

Islington also insist on a high adult/child ratio, working with no more than fifteen children, broken down into small groups for individual classes and activities.

There is great emphasis, in all the projects, on consistency and communication amongst staff. It is a condition of a successful group that the staff can meet regularly for discussion working through their own attitudes, policies and feelings, in order that a consistent pattern of relationships can develop in the groups. It is admitted, however, that this is by no means easy to maintain, and experience of group work, and the discussion and exploration which accompany it, is apt to make the workers themselves very vulnerable. Constant staff communication helps to maintain both a supportive framework and an area in which difficulties can be exposed and worked through.

Supervision and parental contact

We noted before that Wythenshawe regard intermediate treatment as an aid to supervision, and that a condition of accepting cases is that the supervisor should be prepared to participate in the group. This reflects a general concern among the projects that intermediate treatment should not simply be isolated phenomenon in the children's lives, but should, as far as possible, be linked with casework. And we also remarked in the second chapter that, on some interpretations of intermediate treatment, the social worker/supervisor appears to be only minimally involved, "stopping at the door", as it were, of the facility to which he has allocated the child.

The most obvious example of linked treatment and casework occurs with the two residential projects. Northorpe Hall engage in casework with the families during the week and remark that it is essential to link treatment with home life. Dallington Lodge, though initially contact with parents was minimal, have now come to involve themselves in statutory supervision and, like Northorpe Hall, will increasingly make family casework – and family group treatment – an inherent part of the work.

The process appears to be a two-way one. In participating in intermediate treatment with the boys, the staff come to know more about them than one can reasonably expect of the supervisor, unaided. This knowledge is, of course, of great value in the casework situation. Conversely, the knowledge of the family situation can be of help in the intermediate treatment setting: in both directions, there are opportunities for translating and synchronising behaviour and attitudes. Nottinghamshire, indeed, have found cases in which, if a child's supervisor is not involved in the group of which he is a member, the child has come to regard one of the adults in the group *as* his supervisor. Hence, there is now a general orientation towards including the supervisor in the groups where possible. Wythenshawe, of course, operate according to the same pattern. The Youth Development Trust staff do not perform casework themselves, but the supervisors are included in the groups.

The lower key, club-type projects do not have such intensive contact, in general, though Higher Clarence report that when, in times of crisis, visits to families were made, this was usually followed by improved behaviour. The exception is Pontefract, where the full-time workers do engage in family casework. Even here, the operation is most successful where the supervisor uses the club as part of his own casework, and maintains involvement with the boy at the club.

Islington's relation to the family setting may be more problematic, as day-care is, of course, a far more intensive form of provision, and may be perceived by some parents as a threat. The project staff describe the dynamics of the relationship as follows: "If children cannot achieve a strong group identify then the significance of home problems becomes crucial to progress. If we are unable, in turn, to influence family dynamics, our chances of success are minimal. "There is a risk to the family relationships inherent in intensive provisions of this kind, as changes in the child's attitudes may upset the status quo at home. If the child remains at home, however, the problems that are raised can be worked through, with the centre' support, even if this process temporarily upsets the balance of relationships within the family.

Selection Criteria

Not surprisingly, in view of its greater experience, Northorpe Hall has probably the most developed ideas about the boys it can and cannot help, though it describes its selection process as "unsophisticated". It may be appropriate to quote:

"Intermediate Treatment at Northorpe we feel is unsuitable for:

A: Unintegrated children; the giving of primary provisions entails a total life experience, which could not properly be provided during short residential periods.

B: The very rejected child, where continuous to-ing and fro-ing between the home and the treatment centre would reinforce his feelings of rejection.

C: Children where circumstances, or relationships in the home are so pathological that they are strongly detrimental to healthy emotional or psychological development, or where the child is so deeply emotionally disturbed or delinquent, he requires full time treatment or a prolonged period of treatment.

D: Psychotic, severely physically handicapped and those of very low I.Q. We believe, then, that the boys we can trust are boys who are likely to respond to regular short periods away from home, in a warm, secure environment, within which they are presented with a variety of experiences to answer their particular needs. Such boys are those whose experiences have been so limited that their emotional and/or intellectual growth is stunted and who need compensatory experiences in order to grow. They may, for such reasons, be unable to make satisfactory relationships with peers and/or adults. They may lack self-confidence in emotional verbal, social and physical spheres, or they may be boys with strong anti-authority feelings. They will be boys whose home circumstances may be depressing emotionally, materially deprived, anti-social. They will be boys who come from "brittle" rather than the "broken" family, if we define the broken family as one in which relationships no longer exist and the brittle family in which there are relationship ties holding members together as a group, there being potential for development in the casework sense".

Such a developed frame of reference is, as this passage itself suggests, more appropriate to the aims and resources of a residential centre like Northorpe than, for example, community based schemes, or for preventive projects with more flexible membership patterns. In a general sense, the aims and resources of those other projects will as much determine their selection procedures as those of Northorpe Hall determine selection criteria in their case. So the general basis on which children are referred to the various projects is implicit in what has been said about their aims and objectives. There are, however, other parameters bearing on selection.

i The courts.

In the 1969 Act, intermediate treatment is a requirement attached to a supervision order by the juvenile courts. Technically, then (though our scepticism about this has been discussed in previous chapters), intermediate treatment cases are, or will be, court-referred, and as such are a function of the recommendations of the social worker, and the order agreed by the magistrates. As we have already noted, some projects, especially Nottinghamshire, take this very seriously. Preventive work will not stop some children coming before the courts: a major part of intermediate treatment, therefore, is as a sentencing alternative to care. At the limit, this might involve seeing all potential care-order cases as suitable for intermediate treatment in some form.

ii Statutory and voluntary.

Most of the projects considered here are voluntary organisations, operating in more or less closely maintained relationships with the statutory social work agencies. Clearly, then, as intermediate treatment develops, many of these organisations will be relying on the social work agencies for referrals. This implies, to say the least, good communications and understanding between the supervising agencies and the projects themselves – in order that the supervisors have some knowledge and regard for what the projects are trying to do. This is, of course, another reason for encouraging supervisor participation (though we find many of the projects – especially the club-type projects – regretting that they do not get it consistently). Another feature of the Wythenshawe project is designed to improve relations with other agencies even more: each staff member has his own particular area of responsibility in terms of liaison with other agencies — social services, probation, education and so on. Northorpe Hall tend to limit their referrals to the caseloads of social workers with whom good contact has been established and who have shown an understanding of what the work is all about.

iii Self-referrals.

Some of the projects — especially, though not exclusively, the community-based club-type projects — include children who refer themselves and friends of other social work referrals. Haylands specifically try to maintain a balance between these children and the "real" clients, as did Pontefract in the first instance. We might remember, in this connection, the remarks that were made in the first chapter about delinquency and deprivation, and also about "visible" delinquency — as defined by the courts — and invisible delinquency. It is the existence of both that may require a two-pronged attack on the problem — intercepting those children who do reach the courts, but attempting to provide also for those who do not.

iv Perceived problems.

Again, where it seems plausible to tackle one specific problem in the context of intermediate treatment, children who actually face that problem will be referred. We may think here of the Albany single-parent family group and, especially, the Islington project (as we have also noted, however, other projects prefer a balance in the type of problem group members face, rather than an exclusive single problem, as a criterion of membership — Dallington Lodge, Wythenshawe).

v Geographical factors.

The community-based projects clearly work on a geographical basis (this may be, in some cases, a special case of (iv). In addition, Islington operates in liaison with one particular school, as, in the case of their school-based groups, did the Albany.

vi Compulsion.

Certain anxieties have been generated by the "compulsion" element in intermediate treatment, although, in practice, this has proved to be something of a red herring — at least with the present projects. In one or two, however, a certain caution has been apparent. As we saw, the Albany wished to avoid any element of compulsion for the reasons outlined. On the other hand, one anxiety felt by Wythenshawe was that, before the 1969 Act came into effect in Lancashire, the project lacked a certain amount of authority — which may reflect a feeling that compulsion and sanctions, even if, in the final analysis, they are illusory, give the project security. By and large, however, the projects do not seem to have experienced much difficulty: the referrals have been all too keen to participate (witness the anxieties when the groups come to an end). On occasions, in some projects, a little persuasion has been used at the outset, but once the child has begun to participate, no further persuasion has been needed. Finally, most of the projects have tried to maintain good relations with parents, trying to ensure that they too are willing that the child should take part.

Decision making

All the projects try to transfer responsibility for running the groups to the members as a whole and hence to the children. This, however, is not always easy, especially, as Higher Clarence found, with the younger children. For one thing, as we saw earlier, these young people are not, in general, used to the idea that they can themselves determine their activities and interaction with various agencies with whom contact is made. They are more used to being told what to do than asked what they would like to do. The Albany experience was as much of getting the boys to articulate their needs and desires as it was the execution of their wishes. Moreover, the usual experience of these children can be transformed into a defence mechanism, whereby, if those in "authority" take the decisions, and are seen to exercise control, they can be blamed for whatever failures, disappointments and mistakes occur. Therefore, at another level, the democratisation of the groups is an attempt to overcome this kind of reaction.

It is, for these reasons, virtually impossible simply to transfer responsibility to the group from the start. Nottinghamshire, with over two years' experience now, and the Wythenshawe project, both try to increase the amount of responsibility entrusted to the children gradually over a period of time. This is "responsibility" not in the sense of the children being given responsibility for making sure something actually gets done – this is tantamount to being told what to do – but in the true sense of decision-making: deciding what is to be done, by whom, and when. This is as true of the behaviour pattern of the group as it is of the actual programme content and necessary duties, though the first aspect of decision making will be considered at greater length under the next heading, "Authority and control".

There are several problems associated with this process. One is the children's often limited knowledge of the possibilities, or sometimes their exaggerated fantasies about them. It is easy to slide into a situation where the adults in the groups make the suggestions and the children decide on that basis. This, by itself, is a very passive form of decision-making, as some of the projects admit. The adults, of course, as members of the group have every right to make suggestions, but there must also be a process whereby the children are encouraged to explore the possibilities for themselves and invent new, and realistic ones.

Here again, we find something of a difference between the specific groups and the looser, club-type projects, for whom decision-making processes are far more difficult, there being larger numbers, more needs to be satisfied and less group identity. The Haylands project especially seems to have experienced difficulty in this respect, with the boys avoiding attendance at the regular meetings designed to formulate programmes.

These meetings are still held, but less frequently, and discussion now tends to centre on events that actually require discussion. Free choice of the facilities is still available, of course, and the boy's suggestions are acted on where possible; but there remains the feeling that member participation is not as active as it might be.

Higher Clarence also noted the difficulty that the children's suggestions tend to be limited by their experience. After six months, the format for the younger group came to include one particular activity round which a session would be focused, and this, naturally, required more planning on the part of the leaders. The younger the child, clearly, the longer the transfer of responsibility must take.

For the smaller groups, more cohesive planning and discussion, and more structured activities, are possible, though Northorpe Hall makes the point that it is not necessary to cram every session full of "activities" if the group, on occasions, prefers to spend the day in more relaxed fashion. However, it is possible to set aside time for group discussion in these projects, so that activities can be planned and programmes formulated.

At the same time, it may not be desirable to set up discussion in a vacuum, with the formality and artificiality this might entail. Both Wythenshawe and the Albany feel the need for discussion to arise out of situations (compare, in the different setting, the Haylands pattern), rather than try to get the children discussing at a set time, or just for the sake of it. Given that these children are, largely, non-verbal (though verbalisation is to be encouraged), and that they tend to distrust "verbal" agencies, such as schools and social work, this is perhaps as true of discussions planning activity as it is of discussions about their behaviour or their personal and family problems. Verbalisation, that is to say, should perhaps arise out of situations when appropriate, rather than being undertaken for the sake of it, at least in the early stages. When the children become used to the idea of planning their own activities, it may become possible to have particular times at which this group "task" – like any other task – can be executed.

Similarly remarks apply to the Islington project, and here, of course, group planning also takes in lesson material – a special case of "group activities". The Islington experience illustrates the difficulty of having set times for discussion – for example, in the case of weekly meetings to plan a hobbies afternoon. As their report says, the children were at first very threatened by these sessions and, as an exercise in self-determination, it failed, as they refused to take responsibility for making decisions or simply chose an activity not for themselves, but because a particular member of the staff would be doing it with them. Gradually, however, the session seems to have become a success, as the children came to feel more secure. This does appear to reflect a general, and genuine, difficulty in getting the children to articulate their desires (over and above putting them into practice satisfactorily) which may reflect earlier remarks about self-concepts and self-awareness.

Authority and control

A special case of the decision-making process is control of the group's behaviour, a very delicate point in view of the status of intermediate treatment (in the courts' eyes at least) as an anti-delinquency measure. The ideals of democratisation and group discussion apply here, in all the projects, as they do in activity planning, though the looser structure of the club-type projects presents greater problems – or problems in a more limiting context – than do the specific groups. There are several reasons for this.

First, there is the problem of numbers and group identity, noted before, which make disruption less a thing which the group, overall, is able to control. Haylands, Pontefract and Higher Clarence, in their reports, all stress the need for some form of control, eventually, or at some point, more than the other projects. Second, these projects tend to have a greater turn-over of staff, since the larger numbers require correspondingly more adult workers and volunteers and staff departures and arrivals nearly always provoke some form of testing out, as all three note. Third, the more community-based projects may have more contact with other members of the community, and more contact with the agencies that serve it, and in these contacts, tensions are liable to arise, and the expectations of the community risk being unfulfilled. This was certainly the case, at any rate, with Higher Clarence and the Albany.

Overall, however, the atmosphere of all the projects, in accordance with lines suggested in earlier chapters, is permissive. The style of leadership is informal and personalised. This does not mean, however, that the projects are anarchistic. The only problem occurs – and differences emerge – with regard to how norms and controls are introduced.

Higher Clarence suggest that there are two methods of norming: (a) first set the norm, then develop the membership around it; (b) first develop the membership then the norms to meet the needs. This perhaps reflects the above remarks about the club-type projects, where controls tend to come more from the adult and authority figures than from the members themselves. At any rate, we can clarify (b) as: first develop the membership, then norms introduced by adults – and add (c) first develop membership, then allow members, as far as possible, to introduce norms. Whereas all the projects reject (a), it is possible that there is a tendency for the club-type projects to lean towards (b), whilst the specific groups can at least try for (c), with the intention of allowing the norms to emerge, rather than be set.

There are points, nevertheless, at which leader control is inevitable. One possible example of such a point – and certainly a decision which must be faced – is the option of excluding a member from the group, should this appear to be necessary – an inevitable option as the groups are, after all, set up by the leaders. The projects are, however, unanimous in rejecting this option, although Dallington Lodge have used temporary suspension from their activity as a sanction.

There are, times too, at which adult intervention of a more immediate nature seems essential, as most of the projects are willing to admit, but as they also point out, judgement as to whom intervention is necessary is precarious. Again, there are several reasons. One has to decide, somehow, how far a particular sequence of events has learning potential if it is allowed to continue, so that subsequent discussion may be able to mark out is importance, and issues involved. There is the long-term problem of assessing how far one's *own* anxieties about authority and external agencies are at the root of a felt need to intervene, and whether the possible learning experience that might emerge might not outweigh this personal vulnerability. Finally, one has to judge how far the behaviour is, in itself, reasonable, though one's own perceptions and prejudices may lead one to think it not so. Intervention, when it is deemed necessary, takes several forms – and is clearly dependent, to some extent, on the individual concerned. Dallington Lodge use reprimands and forfeiture of privileges; in other cases, it may take a more physical form.

The point about intervention raises another issue which was mentioned briefly in a previous section – that of leadership consistency. For if intervention is to take place, it is clear that the reasons why it does, and the points at which it must, should be agreed by those responsible. Again, the club-type projects are at a slight disadvantage here, in that with larger numbers, both of members and staff, consistency is harder to obtain. Haylands, for example, frankly admit that "the leadership feels unco-ordinated and unclear about aims", a situation only complicated by staff turn-over. But it is not easy in any of the projects, as there are great temptations to slip into complementary or polarised roles (an experience of Nottinghamshire, for example). This is especially true if a hierarchy is allowed to develop in the staff (which is easily transmitted to the members), and which, once set up, is difficult to overcome. Bearing this in mind, Nottinghamshire and Wythenshawe make a point of trying to ensure no staff hierarchy of any kind, and a status of group membership, essentially, for the adults, just as for the children.

The projects, of course, hope that that energetic intervention will be necessary only infrequently, and it is worth examining the ways in which they attempt to ensure this. As we noted before, the authority of the leaders is predicated, ideally, on their own personal qualities, rather than their capacities as social workers, youth leaders, or whatever. Even where controls are introduced, by the leaders, (Higher Clarence, for example) it is felt that an early tolerance, even permissiveness, of atmosphere, in which informal relationships can develop, is of benefit in obtaining commitment to the group before such restrictions are imposed. And the more these restrictions emerge from the various interactions within the group, the better chance there is of the members perceiving them as necessary to the group's functioning. Indeed, Higher Clarence suggests that, at this stage, controls and reprimands sometimes lead to improved relationships. At the very least, all projects try to place controls in the context of "pointing out the consequences of actions" (Haylands) – trying to present rules and regulations, not as arbitrary and imposed by leaders in virtue of their authority, but as reasonable controls necessary to ensure the functioning and continued existence of the group.

In the specific groups, this process can go further, as we saw, in attempting in a more thoroughgoing fashion, to remove responsibility for the control of the group's behaviour onto the group itself. This can be especially successful when group discussion arises out of a particular situation which seems to require it, as before. It is sometimes surprising how successful this operation can be, when the group agrees a solution to disciplinary problem on its own behalf, for example, by an exercise of group responsibility. However, the Wythenshawe experience also suggests the dangers in allowing the group to come to a decision, and then appearing to undermine it: the point of the solution must be to put it into effect. It is sometimes difficult for people (especially external agencies, which we shall discuss in a moment), to accept the concept of "group responsibility", as there is a natural tendency to individualise and scapegoat; to seek out the individual responsible and take action against him. But the concept of group responsibility, where taken up as a solution, can only be an advance: it at least demonstrates a growing self-awareness, and an awareness of the consequences of actions, and the necessity for controls, on the part of the group members; and it can be far more productive than punishment or sanctions – if, for example, taking responsibility means agreeing to make reparation, as a group. Most of the specific group projects have had this experience, and try to encourage it.

The most difficult aspect of control of behaviour, perhaps, relates to contact with external agencies and members of the community, who all, in their various ways, have expectations about behaviour that may not be met. Most of the projects seem to have encountered this problem at some stage or other, though little progress seems to have been made in arriving at a solution to it. One of the most interesting examples comes from the Albany, when the group that had been meeting outside the school finally came to hold sessions in the school for one afternoon a week. It was soon evident that behaviour that could be tolerated in one context was more problematic in another – given the expectations of the school staff. As the project leader remarks, there were three options: let the behaviour continue, and alienate the staff; intervene, and display an allegiance to the school; or take the group out of the school again, and thus avoid the problem. On this occasion, he chose the latter. This is a problem which extends beyond the school context, however, being applicable whenever the group comes into contact with the outside world. In a less concrete way, Higher Clarence faced community hostility for a period during its existence, particularly from the management committee of the youth club premises they were using.

There are no short cuts with this problem. If one is hoping for progress within the group, it may be acceptable to isolate it in the early stages, as the Albany solution suggests, attempting to minimise contact with external agencies for a period until results have been achieved. This is a policy of Eastern Ravens for example, at least in their groups' early stages. After this, very gradually perhaps, contact can be opened up, in the same way that responsibility in general is gradually transferred to the group. In another context, this fits in with those projects whose aim is, eventually, to phase the children into other, more conventional youth services (Haylands, Nottinghamshire, Albany). We have seen before that immediate placements in such agencies may not be very helpful or successful, this being one reason for adopting the small group technique in the first place as providing a protected area in which self-confidence and new norms and attitudes can be built up. This "isolation", therefore, from society at large, as well as the conventional youth services or schools, may not be as undesirable as it at first appears — in the context, at least, of the specific group. Perhaps the Albany experience can be compared to the Islington experience: it does at least suggest that if reintegration takes place too quickly — if the child, that is to say, is put on his own too soon, before the protected atmosphere of the small group situation has had a chance to work — then one risks failure. This is clearly one area in which more thought, and more work, will have to be put in.

5 FINDING DELINQUENTS

In the previous chapter, we discussed the work of each project in relative isolation from the wider issues of social policy. In the next three chapters, we go beyond individual approaches and seek to relate intermediate treatment to the social and political context in which it will take place, and to a theoretical and administrative framework in terms of which it may be conceived: within this framework, it will be presented not simply as one intermediate possibility, but as a whole range, or continuum, of possibilities extending from unsupported placement in the community to intensive short-term and day care. We shall also make suggestions about the resources that will be required in the construction of such a continuum. To begin with, however, we shall consider the social worker's relations with other agencies.

In the first chapter we suggested that the visibility of delinquency depends not only on the existence and activities of the delinquent, but also on public reaction to those activities. In this chapter we discuss some ways of reducing "delinquency" as a social problem which, though they do not amount to "treatment", nevertheless have a direct bearing on the social worker's approach to the problem. If, as we suggested before, intermediate treatment is in part a buffer between delinquent young people and the agents and institutions of social control, the social worker must, through effective negotiation with these agents, create a space in which young people can work through their attitudes and problems.

What we intend to discuss initially is the application of deviancy theory to the delinquency situation in England and Wales, and the important role social workers play in it. At first sight what we have to say may appear irrelevant to intermediate treatment which is, after all, the subject under discussion here. Intermediate treatment is, however, intended for labelled deviants and the process whereby the label "delinquent" attaches itself to a particular child is of unique importance in determining whether or not, and what type of, intermediate treatment is required. Secondly, and of equal importance, is our belief that any anti-delinquency programme must take account of all the variables associated with the creation and discovery of this particular social phenomenon. In this respect, police activity, police procedure, local authority and police liaison, the policies of neighbourhood schools, and the existence of youth facilities – indeed, even the law itself – require scrutiny.

The Courts

By virtue of their training and traditional role, social workers are generally orientated towards personal pathology. The nineteenth century medical-legal model of professional practice continues to dominate the social services despite recent movements in the direction of social action. These influences can be seen in the attitudes many social workers display when dealing with delinquents. When a child is referred by the police for social services investigation, or subject to pre-trial enquiry, the social worker will search for pathology — and, needless to say, he will find it. Using this medical model, social workers will account for delinquency in terms of inadequate socialisation, lack of parental control or attention, or even, in some instances, psychopathology.

It is interesting to reflect in this situation on the recommendations social workers or probation officers make to the juvenile courts. When a child first appears before the court, the recommended sentence is usually low down on the tariff scale and in accordance with a first appearance (conditional or absolute discharge, fine, attendance centre order, supervision order). However, a subsequent appearance will more often than not carry with it a stiffer penalty (supervision order with intermediate treatment requirement, interim care order, etc). The recommendation for more radical intervention will apparently be justified by the discovery of further abnormalities in the child and his family situation, stimulated by the reporting of a further offence. Tariff is operating but it is rationalised by the use of the language of psychopathology. Recent research on probation officers' recommendations would suggest that they also take into account the views and likely sentencing decisions of magistrates rather than the treatment needs of offenders as such.[1]

The 1969 CYPA is a strange combination of legal/judicial and medical/welfare considerations. For example, while juvenile courts are required to give prime consideration to the needs of the child, Section 27 states that "If it appears to a local authority that it is necessary, for the purpose of protecting members of the public, to exercise their powers in relation to a particular child in their care in a manner which may not be consistent with their general duty under Section 12 of the said Act of 1948 to further his best interests and afford him opportunity for proper development, the authority may, notwithstanding that duty, act in that manner". This simple statement perhaps sums up the 1969 CYPA, which at best probably embodies an unhappy combination of criminal and social proceedings and sentences, and at worst is a potentially damaging confusion of both. While the business of juvenile courts is primarily that of the trial and sentencing of young criminal offenders, many of its sentences are carried out by social workers who, after the proceedings, present themselves as 'helpers', though the usual result of court sentences is some form of punishment. This surely cannot make sense to the young people concerned. Nor can it seem just when different sentences are handed out for similar offences. No wonder delinquents are not predisposed to view social work activity favourably.[2]

A further danger exists in Care Proceedings, where it is necessary to prove to the court that the child is "in need of care or control which he is unlikely to receive unless the court makes an order under this section in respect of him". This particular requirement makes clients highly vulnerable. The so-called "care and control test" ought really to be the subject of much closer examination, both in its presuppositions and practice. No reliable care-law has yet been developed to guide magistrates in deciding whether this condition is satisfied in particular cases. While the "offence" condition of care proceedings is predicated on an individual's actions, the "care and control" test focuses on the motives, intentions and dynamics of both individuals and families which are not simple issues especially for courts primarily concerned with offences.

However, the legal context of intermediate treatment does have its positive aspects. Firstly, it gives juvenile courts an extra and much needed sentencing possibility between supervision and care (the original intention of *Children in Trouble*). Secondly, if magistrates are prepared to respond to the challenge presented by intermediate treatment, then they will have an important political role to play in ensuring that local authorities provide comprehensive intermediate treatment programmes. Unfortunately, many of their efforts so far have been employed in criticising local authorities on the issue of residential accommodation for young offenders. One effect of this may have been to reduce the numbers and proportion of non-residential treatment orders made since 1969.

Negotiating with the Police

Approximately 70 – 80% of the children who appear before the juvenile courts charged with criminal offences never come before the court again. Indeed, it can be suggested that a degree of delinquent activity is relatively normal in adolescence. How often has one heard the comment that many of the children appearing before the juvenile courts have merely had the misfortune to be found out? Several studies have been made in the recent past of aspects of youth culture which emerge as delinquency and give rise to comment by the media and generate alarm among the public. We are referring here to published studies on Mods and Rockers,[3] Hell's Angels[4] and adolescent drug-users.[5] It appears that there is a relationship between published, popularised accounts of various types of delinquency, such as drug-use, football hooliganism and "mugging", or violence in schools, and the actual expansion of such activities in so far as the public becomes sensitised and aware of these things, and actually looks for them or notices them more frequently. This process is known as "amplification" and leads more often than not to increased police vigilance and exemplary sentences from the courts which may be out of all proportion to the actions themselves.

The constructive use of police/local authority liaison and effective court representation can, however, go a considerable distance towards modifying this process. Most local authorities have a system whereby offenders under the age of 18 years are reported to them before prosecution. Most of the referrals are dealt with routinely, and in a purely administrative manner by Court Sections, or if a child is known to the social services department, passed on to the appropriate social worker for comment. Such a policy has the effect of maintaining a status quo which operates to the disadvantage of clients by ensuring that many of them will appear unnecessarily before a juvenile court. A court appearance, as the spontaneous remission rate indicates, is probably unnecessary in most cases, and holds the danger of a child acquiring a "delinquent identity" which may lead to other delinquent acts or create an awareness on the part of the police and the school of abnormal behaviour, thereby ensuring further attention and reinforcing of the label. Once the police have discovered that a particular child is delinquent, then he becomes a legitimate target for further investigation. Even if such a child has not committed further offences reported to the police, their knowledge of previous offending inevitably leads them to interview him. The outcome of such an interview may be the discovery of further and hitherto unreported offences — often of a trivial and unimportant nature, associated primarily with normal adolescent behaviour in the neighbourhood — which can lead to yet another court appearance. Hence the importance of the positive use of police referrals, for it is frequently possible to prevent further proceedings by opposing prosecution in such cases and negotiating the issue by informing the police of whatever efforts are being made to help. Until the age of criminal responsibility is raised to 14 years, or juvenile courts are abolished, such activity by social workers will be necessary to ensure that children are protected. The recommendations made by police officers in respect of particular juveniles are often determined by a child's response in the interview situation. If he is sullen, hostile or cheeky, then the outcome may not be in his favour. Unco-operative or defensive parents, poor home conditions, and the extent of neighbourhood delinquency are also factors which are taken into account.

If police policy and activity is a determinant of visible delinquency, then it follows that where the police are particularly active, reported delinquency rates will be high. The reality underlying many instances of reported massive upsurges in delinquency, such as that chronicled in the article "Putting Theory into Practice at Ryehill"[6] is often an intensification of police investigations, either as a result of a random change in policy, or a deliberate decision following public pressure to "crack down". A social worker recently reacted to the knowledge that the police station on his "patch" was acquring a CID officer with the simple statement: "More delinquency". Indeed, police policies at football matches, demonstrations and the like are usually reflected in the number of arrests made, and offenders charged. Social workers are in a position not only to negotiate individual cases where juveniles are concerned, but also to discuss policing policy at a fairly senior level. Items which come to mind are not only football matches, but the use of foot patrols as opposed to panda cars, and the distance of police stations from particular neighbourhoods.

Negotiating with the Schools

It has sometimes been suggested that particular schools generate particular types and quantities of delinquency. Hargreaves found that in the secondary school which was the subject of his research, delinquency rates were high among boys who dissociated themselves from academic success and pupil conformity, the overt goals of the institution:

> "... the school plays an important part in the provision and selection of reference groups by the delinquent. The working-class child does not feel status-deprived relative to others *in vacuo,* but relative to those with whom he has a legitimate right to compare himself ... The school in its streaming system provides a mechanism by which potential delinquents are brought together."[7]

In a recent study comparison was made between secondary schools which drew pupils from the same neighbourhoods. The variations found in delinquency rates between the schools could not be accounted for in any other way than this fact: that some schools for whatever reason generated more delinquency internally than did others:

> "... school rates of boys going on to make at least 3 court appearances also show a wide range, and the higher the court appearance rate of a school, the higher its reappearance rate is likely to be."[8]

If the quality of schooling is an important variable in delinquency, then it becomes necessary to identify those factors within particular schools which produce attitudes and behaviour conducive to delinquency, and discuss them with the school staff in the hope that changes can occur within the institutions. Streaming according to academic achievement has been shown to create delinquent groups in the lower streams:

> "It can be argued that the school plays an important part in providing the conditions necessary for the emergence of a group solution. The school contributes to the genesis of the delinquents' 'problem of adjustment' because it exposes the pupils to the ideology of 'getting on', of social mobility, of hard work and middle class behaviour. The teachers are the propagandists of the values required to succeed. For low stream boys, the school both exposes them to the ideology and simultaneously frustrates and deprives them because they lack the values, attitudes and abilities to succeed in that ideology. It penalises them by denying them privileges and by inducing a sense of

failure and personal worthlessness . . . Further, the boys facing such a problem of adjustment do not have to seek out other boys with the same problem . . . The school in its streaming system provides a mechanism by which potential delinquents are brought together."[9]

Another factor associated with delinquency generation and educational structure is the extent to which poor achievers in the lower working classes dissociate themselves almost completely from the educational system as a whole. The content of school programmes has come under examination recently in the move towards curriculum development, and the presentation of meaningful and realistic education to young people. Concern has also been voiced recently about the incidence of violence and truancy in schools since the raising of the school leaving age. While much of this concern reflects hysteria and amplification by the media, it may also be partly due to an increase in truancy from schools which are not only unable to provide a helpful and satisfactory education, but which by virtue of their size create a degree of alienation. The official peak age for indictable offences was 14 years – the year before leaving school, and in view of the fact that this "peak age" rose from 13 to 14 when the school leaving age was last raised, it may be assumed that the peak age has now moved on to the 15th year.[10] Schools with high rates of staff turn-over have a minimum of pupil-involvement simply because consistent long term staff-pupil relationships do not exist. Particular difficulties exist for teachers in secondary schools in so far as their ability to understand the extent to which their own schools generate delinquency is concerned. Phillipson has said of teachers:

" . . . because they had no yardstick against which to set their own experience, and no accurate knowledge of the situation, whatever the actual rate of delinquency in their school, they typically defined the situation as normal; whether the school had a very high rate, an average, or a very low rate, the teachers, knowing nothing of these differences, had no reason to define the situation as anything else other than absolutely normal. Levels of delinquency were typically defined as 'exactly what one expects in a school (or neighbourhood) like this'.

Their typical beliefs about the aetiology of delinquency complemented and reinforced this definition of normality; the home, the family, 'bad company' were some of the mono-causal scapegoats used by teachers to account for delinquency. As these scapegoats invariably lay beyond the school walls, so all responsibility for this 'problem' of delinquency could be placed elsewhere, usually on parents, police, social workers, or the juvenile court. Very few teachers saw the school as in any way contributing to the patterns of delinquency and as a result, responsibility for action in relation to the problem was conveniently placed elsewhere."[11]

If Phillipson is correct in assuming that teachers, because of the nature of their profession and relationship with the community, are unable to comprehend the contribution of their schools to delinquency generation, then it is important that social workers and intermediate treatment practitioners have effective liaison and discussion with local schools on internal school issues. The Intermediate Treatment Day Care Centres in London Boroughs acknowledge the extent to which schools have responsibility for the broader social behaviour of pupils. Of their own particular centre, and its relationship with local schools, Islington Family Service Unit has said:

> "If the schools feel it is not their role to provide this kind of help (Day Care) to those children alienated from its existing structure, then the treatment of non-attenders will have to become yet another specialised category of help with all the inherent charges of isolation and stigma. But we would not see it as merely an extra job that schools might reluctantly shoulder as their responsibility, but as a vital part of making schools a focal point of local community life rather than the purveyors of an education which is viewed as having only marginal relevance by the majority of its consumers. What is true for the children we deal with, we believe, has relevance for all children: the children will only truly learn what they feel to have relevance for them, emotionally, socially, practically. To view education in isolation from the emotional and social needs of the children is to deprive it of its most powerful source of relevance."[12]

Delinquency is the concern of all professionals who aspire to influence the lives of the young, and teachers will need to engage in dialogue with social workers about policies relating to discipline in schools, staff-pupil relationships, streaming and curriculum development. As with the police, discussion between schools and social workers tends to centre on individual cases, but it is perhaps broader policy issues which require attention if any substantial impact is expected on juvenile crime rates.

Negotiating with Communities

While studying juvenile delinquency in Exeter, C. Bagley discovered that there is a relationship between public expenditure on youth services and juvenile delinquency.[13] Bagley selected 22 towns in England and Wales which were comparable police areas, were physically separate and had populations of between 20,000 and 50,000. The juvenile crime rates in these "smaller conurbations" were compared with other factors such as the proportion of working class people in the town (correlating well with overcrowding, high birthrate, provision of local authority housing, etc) and, in combination, against expenditure on youth services. Youth service expenditure in areas with large working class populations correlated negatively with juvenile delinquency. In fact, the correlation, at – 0.75 is a very high one indeed considering the nature of the material used to effect the statistical analysis. The result of Bagley's study may be represented by the following matrix:

Expenditure on Youth Service	*Working class Population*	*Juvenile Crime*
LOW	LOW	MODERATE
LOW	HIGH	HIGH
HIGH	LOW	LOW
HIGH	HIGH	MODERATE

Bagley concluded that a casual connection existed between high expenditure on youth services in particular towns and the tendency for these towns to have low juvenile crime rates. By expenditure on youth services, Bagley specifically meant:

> "... expenditure per head for the age group 15 to 20 in each county borough ... (on) centres fully maintained by the LEA; on youth officers and organisations; youth leaders, full and part-time; aid to voluntary organisations and other individual youth groups, including salaries of leaders; assistance to county headquarters of voluntary organisations; expenditure on training of leaders and helpers; and on visits abroad, camps, orchestras, use of school buildings etc."[14]

It would appear from this study that if effort is concentrated on youth services in particular areas, it will be rewarded by relatively lower delinquency.

It must be emphasised, however, that the provision of youth clubs and facilities for young people will not necessarily help those who have already come to the attention of social control agencies. Martin Davies[15] found that the use or non-use of leisure activities by the 507 convicted probationers in his study had no relationship with reconviction. The implication of this finding would support our thesis that the provision of youth clubs and facilities for identified and labelled delinquents is of little value in itself and that the experience of delinquency does not predispose the delinquent to make use of such facilities. Rather, Bagley's study suggests that such provision has a place in a programme of delinquency prevention. One writer on intermediate treatment has suggested that the role of facilities listed in the regional plans for Intermediate Treatment should be conceived in just these terms.[16]

In areas of high delinquency, where few if any youth facilities exist then social workers' efforts to create such facilities may pay dividends. Adventure playgrounds, clubs, holiday play-schemes and neighbourhood festivals all have a part to play at the preventive end of the intermediate treatment spectrum. In some communities, political pressure may need to be applied, in others, negotiation with schools may secure the use of school facilities during holidays. Clients themselves have a significant role to play in the creation of neighbourhood youth clubs particularly in very deprived communities.

A Reminder

Perhaps the most important – and for that matter most neglected – item in preventing delinquency is poverty itself. Karl Marx and Frederick Engels developed a consistent theory of the link between poverty and crime over 100 years ago.[17] Since then, numerous studies have, in one way or another, tended to confirm this theory. In 1925, Sir Cyril Burt confirmed that delinquency rates were highest among those families in the population with the poorest material circumstances.[18] Low income and its corrollaries of poor and overcrowded housing, and low social class, correlates overwhelmingly with delinquency. Perhaps the best predictor for any child of a delinquent career would be parental income and social class, associated with quality and quantity of schooling and leisure opportunities. Social workers may spend a lot of time looking for psychological stresses in families which appear to produce delinquents, but perhaps the most important stresses of all are economic in origin. Section 1 of the 1963 CYPA permits local authorities to spend money on preventing children from being received or committed to public care. So far, this legislation has had a very limited and unimaginative application. Increasing emphasis on welfare rights and poverty in general is a welcome change, but unless society itself is capable of an economic restructuring crime will continue to be a normal phenomenon.

"Middle-ranking Agents of Social Control"

The experience of delinquency may dictate that intermediate treatment takes a "treatment" form in so far as it inevitably focuses on individual labelled deviants who, because of a variety of deprivations, have assumed values, attitudes and a type of anti-social behaviour which it takes skilled and carefully structured group work to change. For those who have not yet experienced such a phenomenon or acquired a firm label from a court, much can be done to prevent such a process occurring. The type of education available, the quality and quantity of leisure opportunities and general social and economic factors all require attention. It has to be recognised, however, that the deviant/deviancy controller interface is a critical and legitimate area for the formation of a rational policy by social workers. Police activity and social work liaison has received little academic and research attention despite the creation of the Police Juvenile Bureau and local authority Court/Police Liaison Departments since 1969. As Becker has said:

> "The interactionist approach shows sociologists that a major element in every aspect of the drama of deviance is the imposition of definitions – of situations, acts, and people – by those powerful enough to

sufficiently legitimated to be able to do so. A full understanding requires the thorough study of those definitions and the processes by which they develop and attain legitimacy and taken-for-grantedness."[19]

Social workers assume that children reported to them by the police are "essentially" delinquent – that is to say their delinquency is their most important personal attribute, while other qualities can go completely unrecognised. The processes whereby children acquire this type of deviant identity urgently need investigation and clarification. Cautioning rates for juvenile offenders vary from less than 12% to over 60%.[20] What do these figures show? Do they reflect two types of policy both within police departments and within their respective social service departments?

The 1969 CYPA has given power to social workers to act as "middle-ranking agents of social control."[21] They now have the opportunity to intervene in the process of defining delinquents, and it is hoped that they will act positively and responsibly to this challenge.

6 A CONTINUUM OF CARE

The analysis in Chapter 4 was of a number of projects in different areas experimenting with intermediate treatment in a variety of ways. Having tried, in this analysis, to draw out some of the approaches and techniques that can be used in intermediate treatment, we discussed the negotiations that may be conducted by social workers with other agencies. What we have not so far tried to do, however, is place intermediate treatment in the general context of social policy. How is intermediate treatment related to other forms of provision for young people? In this chapter, we try to answer this question by offering an interpretation of the idea that intermediate treatment is intermediate between those forms of treatment "which involve complete removal from home and those which do not."[1] The structure we develop according to this interpretation is of a "continuum of care".[2]

All children have certain basic facilities available to them. These include not only specific provisions such as youth clubs, playgrounds and activity centres, but a variety of other settings of which they can make use: streets, parks, cafes, shops, school grounds and buildings – in fact, the entire social architecture of their environment. Schools themselves are in a slightly different case since attendance at them is obligatory. However, we might still regard them, with the others, as basic, or "universal", provisions in the sense that all children may (or must) make use of them.

A minority of children are unable to make use of these facilities in a socially acceptable way. Theft, vandalism, disruptive behaviour and truancy are all instances of that break-down in relations between basic provisions and the juvenile population that we refer to as delinquent. We take it that many, perhaps most, delinquent children are, in various ways, disadvantaged or deprived, and that this is, in an important sense, the reason that they do not conform in their use of the facilities in question.

Their inability to do so tends to increase their disadvantage. Exclusion from, or indifference to, the various provisions, self-exclusion from school, lack of opportunity to form associations with those, of all ages, who might be able to help in their development – these can only serve to increase the social distance between these children and their contemporaries. This is especially obvious in the case of schools, but is also true of all other provisions which contribute, no matter how informally, to adolescent social education. There is a vicious circle in which disadvantage limits ability to make use of basic provisions, and inability to make use of basic provisions leads to an increase in disadvantage.

As a result, some children come to the notice of the control and welfare agencies, and of these, a significant proportion end up in residential care. Approved schools, borstals and detention centres are the last resort of the penal system for juveniles, special provision for those who are deemed unfit to remain in the community, or unlikely to receive the care and control they require there. However, as *Children in Trouble* pointed out, the step of placing a child in this form of care is a drastic one, particularly in cases which might be regarded as borderline. The gap between "those forms of treatment which remove the child from his home and those which do not" is a very wide one. It is the gap that the concept of intermediate treatment was designed to bridge.

Although intermediate treatment was designed as a sentencing possibility between the two extremes, definition and exposition in official literature left several questions unanswered. To take one of the several dimensions, while *Children in Trouble* and the two D.H.S.S. publications talk of "brief, regular contact with a different environment" as a chief aim of intermediate treatment, there is, despite the thirty days stipulation (which we have already suggested to be arbitrary in itself), little indication as to how often such contact should take place, how long it should continue, or how long each session might be. While this was in the interests of greater flexibility, the limited response of the planning authorities and the restricted interpretation of intermediate treatment that has gained currency suggest that further elaboration is necessary. What is needed is a framework in terms of which such questions can be asked and answered and within which various facilities and projects, such as those we have already discussed, can be located.

Between the basic or "universal" provisions and residential care, there is a theoretically indefinite number of possible provisions, varying not only in intensity and regularity of treatment but also in style of work, staffing and social work components. Since different children would need to be placed at different points in this spectrum, a coherent plan of intermediate treatment would require the development of a comprehensive range of these possibilities. If this were to happen, intermediate treatment would become, not a single type of provision intermediate between supervision and residential treatment, but a *continuum of care* with supervision and residential treatment as its extreme points or limiting cases. This small, but significant, conceptual shift is illustrated in diagram (a).

To construct a continuum of care would be to make the style and intensity of a range of provisions of central importance. This would be in contrast to the current regional plans which are intended, in some measure, to represent the range of possibilities available for intermediate treatment. For the facilities listed in the plans are categorised in terms of merely contingent features (such as responsible body, admissions procedures and financial arrangements) rather than according to intensity and style of treatment method, which are the quantitative and qualitative features of the continuum of care.

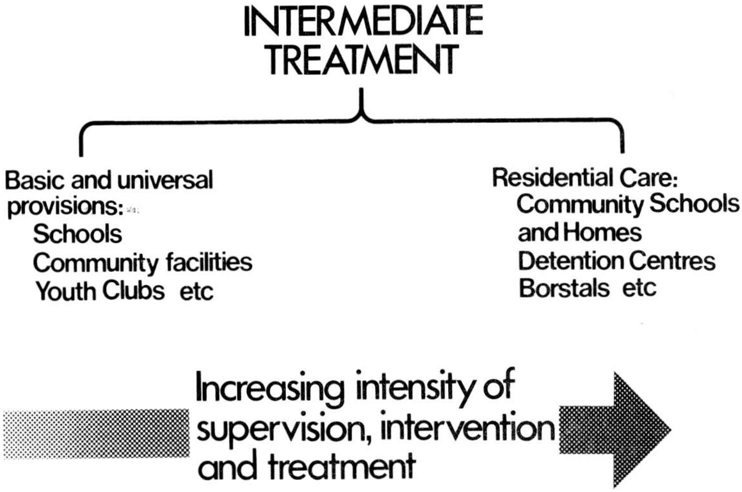

A continuum of care, then would embody a number of different facilities, varying in style and intensity, and so related as to provide a comprehensive scheme, ranging from once-a-week placements in a local youth club right up to highly intensive day-care. Below, we give an example which represents a series of cross sections through a continuum of care. Each stage represents a possible programme within the total range of the continuum, increasing in intensity of intervention and treatment, an intensity measured in terms of time factors, treatment medium, staffing and social work components. The several stages are not, however, fixed points on a scale, but cross-sectional examples from the indefinite number of possibilities characterising the continuum. The use of basic provisions in low key treatment and preventive work represents a change of emphasis from the general impression of intermediate treatment that has gained currency, and which we criticised in Chapter 2.

Possible stages of a continuum of care

Stage 1. Basic and universal provisions available to all children, for example schools, local youth facilities and other amenities.

Stage 2. Youth facilities used on a "referral" basis; placement in an appropriate setting (much as on the "official" view of intermediate treatment).

Stage 3. Specialist youth club catering specifically for disadvantaged and delinquent children. One, two or three evenings a week. High adult-child rate. Youth workers, volunteers and social workers. Supervisor involvement where possible.

Stage 4. Local treatment groups, run by supervising social workers, or by youth workers with supervisor participation. Number of young people in any group lower than numbers involved at Stage 3. Weekly meetings, using locally available equipment, facilities and volunteers.

Stage 5. Local treatment group as at stage 4. Meets residentially for up to six weekends in a year and arranges holiday courses in which supervisors may also participate.

Stage 6. Local treatment group as at stage 4. 45 days aggregate residential per year. Group begins with a block week in residence, followed by at least one weekend every month and a block week every six months.

Stage 7. Local treatment group. Highly intensive supervision and family casework by specialist social workers. Three nights a week, and three weekends out of four. Night stay facilities and block residential periods. Work with parallel parents groups.

Stage 8. Short-term care (maximum of three months). Short-stay therapeutic community.

Stage 9. Day care. Highly intensive supervision and family casework. Educational provisions on a free school model. Specialist staff include teachers and trade instructors as well as social workers. Work with parallel parents group.

Stage 10. Full-time residential care.

It should be emphasised again that, though each stage illustrated here represents an increasing intensity of intervention and treatment, these are only examples selected from an indefinite number of possibilities. Nor should it be assumed that any single facility will embody only one of these stages. As we have suggested before, some projects may span two, or even three, stages of the continuum, working in different ways with different groups of young people, though membership of these groups may often overlap. Such overlapping will facilitate the movement of children up and down the continuum, which is another of its essential features.

The conceptual shift to the continuum of care suggests that intermediate treatment, far from being one of three possibilities, absorbs nearly all the possibilities. It would be possible, theoretically, to place any child at some point within the continuum that falls short of full-time residential care. Thus, the problem of assessment is no longer one of determining whether a particular case is suitable for intermediate treatment, but one of determining which form of intermediate treatment is appropriate – that is, at what point on the continuum a child can best be placed. This assessment process may take place within the continuum itself, perhaps most conveniently at stages 3,4 or 5.

Movement within the continuum is a permanent possibility. Once the child has entered the continuum, the objective will always be to prevent a drift to the upper end (residential treatment) and effect a return, as swiftly as possible, to the lower end (basic provisions, unplaced and unsupervised), although it may sometimes be necessary to intensify treatment for certain children. In this context, residential treatment really is a last resort for children who have not responded to the attempt to slow down their upward progress through the continuum. A more detailed discussion of assessment for, and movement within, the continuum will be found towards the end of this chapter.

Planning

The framework for planning recommended by the D.H.S.S. and adopted almost universally by the Children's Regional Planning Committees gives very little indication of the quality and quantity of treatment that might be offered by the listed facilities. We have already suggested that, in their present form, the regional plans could be abandoned. But it might be possible to amend them according to the requirements of a continuum of care. An amended scheme would be different in three basic ways. First, it would be a good deal shorter, as facilities would be incorporated into it only if they were integrated into a planned continuum. Second, the plan would in fact be a plan and not a list. The aim would be to construct a comprehensive range of treatment facilities, and to fill the gaps by creating new ones, so that the plan's framework would not simply be a record of facilities already available but also a blueprint for development. Thirdly, the scheme would be more detailed, as each facility would be described in such a way as to bring out its location within the continuum and its contribution to the overall treatment plan.

How the theoretical model of a continuum of care might take on such a planning profile is illustrated in Appendix B, which does, in fact, amount to a modified regional scheme. Not only does it incorporate the contingent features of each facility such as name, location, responsible body, etc., it also indicates the style and intensity of intervention and treatment.

The columns variously headed "Youth Club", "Specialist Club", "Local Treatment Group", "Local and residential treatment group", "Short-term care" and "Day care" represent location within the continuum. Under "Programme" would be entered the activities available in each facility. It would not, of course, be possible to itemise these in detail, but general categories could be coded in the following way:

a) general indoor activities
b) general outdoor activities
c) general social facilities
d) educational activities
e) adventure activities
f) work training
g) therapeutic

h) community service
i) arts and crafts

It should be noted that the therapeutic element (g) represents a way of exposing the child in a group structure. It is not just the use of discussion and socio-drama (for example), but also a framework in terms of which other activities are organised.

Ideally, perhaps, continuum units would be set up on a neighbourhood basis, in keeping with the idea that the child should be treated in the environment and locality from which he originates. Thus, if overall planning continued on a regional basis, an area code would also be needed in order that gaps in provision could be identified, and adequate facilities developed, on a local or neighbourhood basis.

Facilities at various stages in the continuum illustrated above could be entered accordingly into the planning profile. For example, a facility at stage 2 would have its time factors (in this case, the evenings it was open, and the period of time it was open for) entered under the "Youth club" heading. It would have a relatively low staff-child ratio (perhaps 1:20) and involve a fairly high number of children. There would be little in the way of social work component, as the club leaders would have no special responsibility for family casework, or liaison with schools and police. The range of its activities would be something like a/b/c, coded as above.

A facility at stage 3 would have time factors entered under the "Specialist club" heading. It would have a higher staff-child ratio (say 1:4) and have a restricted membership, limited, unlike the youth club whose members "refer themselves", to social work referrals. Supervisor participation and involvement would be encouraged, thus forming a link with casework. The range of activities available would be similar to that of a normal youth club.

Other stages in the illustrative continuum could also be entered in a similar way. As an example of these later stages, five of the projects described in Chapter 3 have been located within this planning framework, their various features tabulated appropriately. These projects are not, of course, situated in the same area; but, taken together, they begin to form the outline of a possible continuum of community care (Appendix B).

The essential features of the continuum may be summarised as follows:

a) It represents an increasing intensity of intervention and treatment between the two polarities of basic provisions ("prevention") and full-time residential care.
b) It offers something to all disadvantaged children regardless of the way in which their needs present to society, whether it is as a young offender, or a child in need of care, control and protection.
c) It offers a facility to the juvenile courts as a sentencing possibility.
d) It is a dynamic model of social work intervention in that it allows the movement of children within it, acting both as a buffer between children at risk and institutional care, and as a means of rehabilitating children already in care.

Assessment

The effect of the model of the continuum of care is to make of intermediate treatment a range of intermediate possibilities, rather than a single provision, midway between basic provisions and residential care. This, as we mentioned before, has implications for assessment. As long as intermediate treatment is seen as one of three fundamental sentencing possibilities in a tariff system (supervision, intermediate treatment, and care) it will appear to be appropriate for a particular range of cases — a middle range. The problem of assessment is then one of determining this middle range: for which children is intermediate treatment suitable? But if intermediate treatment is a continuum, which embodies the whole range of possibilities, with supervision and residential treatment as its extreme cases only, it is transformed into a possibility for all, or most children, since young people can be moved up and down the continuum as the need arises.

On what grounds, then, are we to determine the point of entry in any given case? We take it that there are two essential dimensions in which factors may be located: the perceived needs of the children concerned, and their visibility as deviants.

The first of these dimensions concern the child's social environment, the problems perceived within a family, a neighbourhood and a situation of general poverty and deprivation. Educational and psychological needs and abnormalities of various kind, along with relationship distortions would also be classified as "perceived needs". The second dimension is a function of interaction with various social agencies such as the police, social workers and courts (delinquency), and education welfare (truancy).

Diagram (b) shows how these dimensions relate to assessment and selection for intermediate treatment. The diagram illustrates how the point of entry of any given child on the continuum of care is determined theoretically by his or her location on a spectrum of perceived needs and deviant visibility.

It is not suggested, of course, that there is an exact correlation between the level of need and the level of deviant visibility. The child's penal career will more often than not be determined by the extent to which he is known to the police and courts, rather than the extent to which he is thought to come from a disadvantaged background. Whether or not a child becomes subject to a Care Order, or avoids one, usually depends on the number of previous appearances, his relations with the police and social work agencies, and the gravity of the offence. We might suppose, therefore, that the point at which a child enters the continuum of care, and the intensity of supervision and treatment he initially receives, would in most cases be determined by visibility factors rather than need factors. In many cases only if the magistrates and police can see that certain intensive measures are being taken (up to day-care, for example) will it be likely, that a care order can be avoided. For a child with a record of court appearances, the courts may well feel that referral to a youth club, as part of his intermediate treatment, just would not be enough (perhaps rightly so), and a care order might be recommended unless the system were sufficiently flexible — along the lines developed here — to enable more intensive measures to be adopted. Hence, in general terms, the level of intensity will be determined by the child's deviant visibility. This is not to say, however, that once the child has been assimilated into the continuum, his progress within it will not be affected by other variables — in particular, his needs and relationships as perceived by the workers concerned. In other words, while starting at a fairly high-intensity point in the continuum, an entry determined by visibility, he may fairly quickly proceed to a lower level, if his needs are not desperate and his relationships with peers, adults and authority figures not too distorted. Such a system of selection and assessment would also have the advantages that both the delinquent and society would see justice being done: at least initially, the more trouble a child gets into, the more intensive is the supervision he is likely to receive.

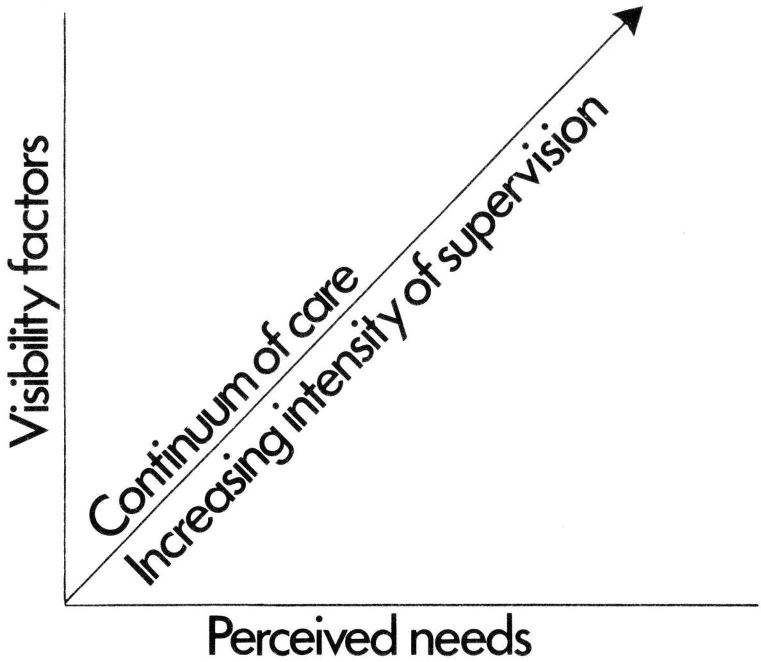

We have so far discussed the continuum in terms of referral from the courts — as intermediate treatment is, at least to begin with, a sentencing possibility. It is clear, however, that this is not the only pattern of referral. The experience of the projects we have discussed, and that of some local authorities, suggest other possibilities. For, particularly at the lower end of the continuum, there is ample room both for self-referrals and referrals from social work agencies that are not a direct consequence of a court appearance. We have shown how some of the projects described in Chapters 3 and 4 (placed at points of lower intensity on the continuum) cater for a mixture of children — some referred by social work agencies, some self-referred and some referred by friends. These projects have ways of working with children that are the same regardless of the way in which they arrived at the facility. This pattern is easily accommodated to the continuum. Children do of course already "refer" themselves to stage 1, because these facilities are intended for all. Similar types of facility are used in stages 2 and 3. This is, then, something we can expect to happen: children entering the continuum as a result of processes other than court appearances. In the nature of things such entries will be made at the lower end of the continuum, while entries from court will tend to be at the higher end. However, children who decide to attend intermediate treatment facilities of their own volition, and who are completely unknown to social work agencies may have unmet needs. In such a case, a child referring himself could be passed on to a more intensive framework subject to his agreement. The same organisations or projects can, of course, represent various points on the continuum. We have seen how Pontefract, for example, is thinking of doing work that would fit both the lower end of the continuum (stage 2 and 3) and also work that would correspond to stages further up (e.g. stage 5). Within this context, of course, entry and progress within the continuum would be simple.

Casework

A subject that has occasionally been discussed before, is the relation between intermediate treatment and casework with families. It was suggested that the experience of the projects has been that the closer these are the better. Some of the projects actually do their own casework. It seems likely that the continuum of care will have to include or be associated with various forms of work with families. This work will probably vary as the intensity of work with the child varies (note the difference in relationships with families experienced by the lower-key projects and by the Islington Centre). Roughly, as the intensity of work with the child increases, so must intensity of work with parents: changes in the child have an effect on the family which it may not, without help, be able to assimilate. One suggestion might be to extend the group work style to the families themselves and have parallel parents groups – parallel, that is, to the main continuum. Group work with families and parents is not entirely new in social work, but the continuum might provide an opportunity to harness it to work with the children.

Another, and perhaps, even more important consideration here, is the relationship between the child and his supervisor. If the supervisor is responsible for casework with the child then the quality of the casework relationship, as experience seems to have indicated, will be considerably improved. If, therefore, the more intensive types of intermediate treatment are actually undertaken by the supervisor, then the benefit of a closer relationship will serve to maximise its potential.

7 BEGINNING INTERMEDIATE TREATMENT

In the final chapter, we shall make suggestions about the development of intermediate treatment, as a continuum of care, in the legal and administrative context of the last three or four years. We shall examine briefly the role of the various services and the repsonse of the courts and social services departments to the 1969 C.Y.P.A.; and we shall discuss the organisation of resources to meet the demands of a system of non-residential community care.

Responsibilities

At the present time, firm statutory responsibility for intermediate treatment lies only at the two ends of what we have described as the continuum of care. The education department, together with many voluntary organisations, provide "basic" facilities for young people in general, and social services departments provide residential care. There is, of course, no single agency which can be considered responsible for the medium to high intensity forms of treatment located in the middle of the spectrum. It is, perhaps, no coincidence that of the ten projects described in Chapter 3 only one is run from within the mainstream of a social services department (Nottinghamshire). Though most of the others are funded, directly or indirectly, through the local authorities, they are, to varying degrees, independent as regards policy and method. However, as we suggested in Chapter 2, there are funds of knowledge, skill and resources deposited in all the statutory agencies, including the Probation Service which, perhaps to a greater extent than the local authorities, has years of experience with delinquents and their families. The problem is how to bring these skills and resources together in a workable, flexible system of intermediate treatment.

The responsibility for financing intermediate treatment lies with the local authority. Section 18(4) of the 1969 Act states:

> "Where a supervision order requires compliance with such directions as are mentioned in section 12(2) of this Act, any expenditure incurred by the supervisor for the purposes of the directions shall be defrayed by the local authority of which the area is named in the order in pursuance of subsection (2) of this section."

In the case of children who have not appeared before a juvenile court, the local authority has enabling powers to cover expenditure on a variety of activities under Section 1 of the 1963 C.Y.P.A. This is, of course, how the projects we have described are financed, together with voluntary contributions from various sources. Unfortunately, however, some local authorities have seen intermediate treatment strictly in terms of court orders, and the financing of their schemes has been restricted to funds derived from the 1969 Act. Since another condition of this Act is the use of facilities in the regional schemes, the poverty of the latter has resulted in a low number of intermediate treatment requirements; this may, in turn, lead to a reduction in financial provisions made under the Act. This can only reinforce the marginality of intermediate treatment: without orders, money cannot be released; and without money, intermediate treatment cannot be developed. The first step in resolving this impasse might be, as we have suggested before, to combine money from both the 1963 and the 1969 Acts to form an "intermediate treatment fund".

Many local authorities, it is true, have been imaginative and generous with 1963 Act provision which, in recent years, have included playgroups for pre-school children, adventure playgrounds and holiday schemes for older children. Similarly, the probation service has been holding annual summer camps for delinquents, an experience which undoubtedly helped to shape the concept of intermediate treatment. Why, then, were the compulsory powers associated with the 1969 Act introduced at all? The plain fact of the matter appears to be that, in principle, there is nothing to intermediate treatment which could not have been done under section 1 of the 1963 Act. Indeed, it could have been done more easily, since the financial conditions laid down in the 1969 Act are restrictive rather than enabling. As David Haxby has pointed out:

> "Local authorities and Regional Planning Committees must be given guidance so that they no longer confine their schemes to the narrow terms of the (1969) Act, and so that they can make provision for the increased expenditure under section 1 of the 1963 Act. The 1969 Act is inert even for translating the intentions of the White Paper into legislation since it relates both schemes and finance to the issuing of directions. Many would say that when *that* point has been reached, the benefits from intermediate treatment are likely to disappear."[1]

The 1969 Act is probably best interpreted as an attempt to goad local authorities slow to take advantage of the 1963 Act into further action. The evidence seems to suggest, however, that the attempt has not really succeeded, and that the issue has in fact been complicated by the harnessing of intermediate treatment to court proceedings.

At the same time, it might be possible to use the directive powers of the juvenile courts to advantage, for, in effect, the courts can now pressurise local authorities into spending money on preventing children from coming into care by means of intermediate treatment requirements. This, however, presupposes a commitment to intermediate treatment on the part of both magistrates and social workers, and it is not clear that there is, in fact, such a commitment. For one thing, social workers, confronted only with the regional plans, have felt unable, or disinclined, to take advantage of the political possibilities. The research already referred to[2] suggests that in some areas there may be both uncertainty and unease about the whole thing. Nor is it clear that magistrates view intermediate treatment or the other provisions of the 1969 Act, with any great favour.

These points may be illustrated by criminal statistics for the years 1971 and 1972, when many sections of the Act first came into operation.[3] These do appear to indicate that the Act is not being used as it was intended to be. For example, it was a primary aim of the Act to encourage the use of care proceedings, rather than criminal proceedings, for cases involving the committing of an offence; hence the importation of the offence condition in section 1(2)(f). However, it would appear that care proceedings are not yet being used in this way. In 1971, 81 children (up to the age of 17) were subject to care proceedings on the offence condition, out of a total of 4021 (about 2%). In 1972, the overall total for care proceedings rose to 4136 – but the number of cases involving the offence condition actually dropped to 55 (about 1.3%).

There are also signs that magistrates, wary of the general trends embodied in the Act, have responded to it by increasing the number of Detention Centre Orders and recommendations for Borstal training – rather than hand certain young people over to the care of the local authority. Thus in 1972, the number of boys aged between 14 and 17 committed to Detention Centres was 440 more than in the previous year. This represented an increase of about 29% (although there had been a slight drop between 1970 and 1971). Similarly, in 1971, there was a rise in the number of boys aged 15 or 16 who were sent on to a higher court from the juvenile court with a recommendation for borstal training. The number increased by 177, representing an increase of about 25% over the proceeding year. These figures are not, of course, conclusive, but they do suggest that the supposition that magistrates, in general, do not admire the 1969 Act is not far wrong.

Social Services

As a result of the 1970 Local Authority Social Services Act, the Children's, Health and Welfare Departments were reorganised to form the new generic social services departments. Most of these departments have adopted the Brunel management model, which incorporates at least four separate sub-divisions within each department. The first of these has responsibility for "field" services – the casework performed by social workers and all functions of the department concerned with advice-giving and counselling. This division has a very limited responsibility for services which are not "professional", even where residential social work is included; nor does it determine the use of cash and kind resources. The second division assumes responsibility for "bricks and mortar", property, food and material items in the residential sector, including the planning and creation of new facilities. The third deals mainly with domiciliary and community services such as home helps, occupational therapy, aids and adaptations for the elderly and physically handicapped and day-care for all client groups. The fourth section is normally concerned with the management of administrative and financial services, accounting, staffing, typing and filing.

Intermediate treatment does not appear to fit comfortably under any of these headings. The professional task is firmly located in "field" services, but the facilities required would be better organised within the residential division, while the nature of the operation as such lends itself to classification as a domiciliary or community-support service. No one division within social services is likely to be able to provide all the professional, financial and material resources needed to develop intermediate treatment, and in some respects we feel that the construction of a continuum of care presupposes a structure which more closely resembles the old children's departments: an analogous structure within the generic social services would not necessarily negate the intentions of the Seebohm Report, upon which the legislation of 1970 was based. In the absence of such an analogue, however, we shall continue to base our observations on the structures that already exist.

In response to the coming into effect of the regional schemes, most departments are appointing intermediate treatment officers, though individual briefs appear to vary from actual involvement to administrative and financial functions. Moreover, they are sometimes limited by an authority's interpretation of intermediate treatment: for example, in many cases there is a duty to liaise with the various facilities listed in the regional schemes, a duty which, as we suggested in Chapter 2, is an inessential and somewhat pointless one. Not so inessential would be liaison with facilities actually making some contribution to a coherent plan of treatment and integrated into a continuum of care. This would not simply be "liaison" however, since responsibility for developing the continuum, for mapping out programmes, for locating buildings, recruiting workers and obtaining equipment, would presumably devolve on the intermediate treatment officer. He would be essentially a development officer: an organiser, initiator and contact-maker. He would be located in the "fieldwork" or professional division of the department, but with free access, perhaps through assistants, to residential and domiciliary divisions to enable the acquisition of financial and material resources. He would be assisted in the construction of a continuum by a permanent enabling committee, a generic committee made up of representatives of social services, education, youth service and probation service. In make-up, such a committee would resemble the working parties appointed by the Regional Planning Committees to investigate and list the facilities available for intermediate treatment in their respective areas. Their role, however, would be rather different in that they would, within the services represented, assist the intermediate treatment officer in promotion, recruitment and training, and in the stimulation and construction of an integrated treatment programme. In brief, their role would be an active, stimulative one rather than a passive, recording one. The Regional Planning Committees themselves might also take on a more positive role: perhaps the task of overall integration within a region. Since their major responsibility has been the setting up of the community home system, their role would have a bearing more on the upper reaches of the continuum, and the creation of facilities linked with, but falling short of, full-time residential care. None of these suggestions is very revolutionary: they merely represent a change of emphasis from a passive to an active role, and from listing and contacting to stimulating and constructing.

Organisation of Resources

Facilities for intermediate treatment at the lower end of the continuum are already in existence — witness the regional schemes. Medium to high intensity facilities, however, particularly those which assume either supervisor involvement or specialist, full-time intermediate treatment social workers, are virtually non-existent. Yet it is for such facilities that the need is most obvious. The problem will be to organise existing resources in such a way as to make the construction of this segment of the continuum possible. In these terms, there is a difference between the upper and the lower ends of the continuum. There are various resources at the disposal of different groups and organisations within the community. At the lower end of the continuum, these resources are deployed in the way in which they are already deployed by those organisations — a young person is placed in, and makes use of, a youth service facility in exactly the same way as any other club member. At the higher end of the continuum, however, resources — often the same resources — are deployed in a different way, according to the requirements of the programme at a given stage: a youth centre may be used as a meeting place for a local treatment group, and club workers may be involved as group workers, in a more highly intensive setting than that of the club. This distinction between two patterns of deployment of resources has been referred to as the distinction between the "allocation" and the "focalisation" models.[4]

In the middle of the continuum, then, available resources are "focused" on the treatment groups. The supervising social worker, or probation officers, may draw up a list of community resources: buildings where meetings and activities take place, such as church halls, club premises, schools, sports halls, theatres, skating rinks, even area social services offices. Youth clubs can provide youth leaders, experienced in working with small groups of children. Equipment for camping, mountaineering, canoeing, sailing, painting, drama, and indoor and outdoor sports can usually be borrowed from schools or clubs. Volunteers can be used to lead activities where expertise is demanded — for clay-modelling, socio-drama, painting, and outdoor pursuits. In this way, three social workers can bring to a small group of nine or ten children a wealth of experience, not only in terms of activity, but also in terms of relationships.

The cost of running such a group (for example, one at stage 5 in the continuum) would be about £500 for a year. This sum would be sufficient to pay for food, accommodation and transport for a group of ten children and three adults in sessions spread out over thirty days. It includes incidental expenses such as the cost of admission to swimming pools and cinemas.

At the present time, very few local authorities and probation services employ social workers specifically to work with small groups of adolescents. Hence, most of the group work performed in these agencies is done by social workers in their spare time. In middle range local treatment groups, we may expect this to continue. It should be recognised that even if the supervising social worker does not himself run the group, he will need to spend at least three or four times as long as individual cases – co-ordinating, selecting, and communicating – as he would in a straightforward supervision situation. When, however, the supervisor participates, evening and weekend work will require compensation for both him and his colleagues. Vague arrangements for time off in lieu are insufficient where full caseloads are carried – not the least reason being that social workers tend not to take time off in any systematic way when immediate pressures are present. Rather, it would be more satisfactory either to make payments of overtime, or grant extra annual leave. In the case of a social worker agreeing to participate in a group for a twelve month period, the local authority could make an offer of either 30 days' pay, 30 days' additional annual leave, or some combination of payment and leave. The authority may then need to employ extra staff to ensure that nothing is lost through intermediate treatment commitments.

The greater the intensity of treatment, the higher the staffing costs would be. At present-day rates, for example, a 30-day group at stage 5 would cost approximately £550 per year in staff over-time, making the total cost of a stage 5 group about £1,050 per year. A stage 6 group would cost roughly £2,000 per year in total, though extra staff would be needed to work in the community to cover the gap created by some social workers bearing relatively smaller and more specialised, caseloads.

These, then, are some of the ways in which medium-intensive intermediate treatment can be supported through existing resources. The most exciting possibility offered by the continuum of care, however, is that of highly intensive supervision used as an alternative to residential care – the upper stages of the continuum. We shall discuss this possibility in the next section.

An alternative to residential care

The Islington F.S.U. Intermediate Treatment Centre is an anti-truancy project, but its potential as a model for alternatives to full-time care is obvious. Day-care centres, catering for small groups of up to 15 children, are rapidly becoming a reality in London where truancy rates are very high. Moreover, day-care is much cheaper than institutional care, currently the only available resource in the case of school non-attendance. The cost of maintaining children in institutions, in both financial and psychological terms, is enormous.

With community schools currently costing over £2,500 (and in London up to £3,500) per child, per year, and doubts being expressed about their effectiveness, the time has come to explore alternatives. The Islington Centre's running costs in 1973 were £12,000. Had the fifteen children attending the Centre been in community schools in the London area, they would have cost the rate-payer something like £52,500. The time has come to give serious consideration to a drastic reduction of the community school population. The saving involved in discharging only ten children from care would more than pay for the purchase and staffing of a day-care centre.

It may, at this point, be relevant to discuss at greater length reservations about the effectiveness of residential treatment, of community schools, detention centres and borstals. There is a basic, and as yet unresolved, dilemma in providing residential care and treatment for offenders, perhaps best summarised by the following extract from *Community Schools Gazette:*

> "This is the logical muddle in his daily tasks. They are called upon to be agents of punishment in so far as they are the visible persons who deprive the child of his or her liberty, freedom of will, and customary environment; at the same time, they are agents of therapy who, by fostering a close relationship and applying the best teaching of social science as they understand it, are striving to cure the psychological illness which they believe to be the cause of delinquency. I am suggesting that this basic paradox inevitably militates against success".[5]

The dual aims of residential care – custody and treatment – cannot easily be reconciled. Indeed, when these two factors are considered separately, it can be seen that community schools are not particularly successful with either. The past 18 years have seen a rapid rise in the numbers absconding from such institutions – in 1968 alone there were approximately 11,000 absconscions.[6] In 1970, 558 boys appeared before courts charged with offences committed during their period of training at approved schools: at the time, the total approved school population was only 7,150. In his recent book on community schools, Norman Tutt says:

> "The effectiveness of rehabilitation on post-institutional behaviour (for delinquents) can be estimated by the well-known 'success rates' of approved schools, detention centres and borstals. The 'success rate' is based on the number of children found guilty of an offence during a

three year follow-up. For the approved schools in the last five years for which statistics are available, from 1963 to 1967, the figures make depressing reading; the average percentage of reconvictions for boys was 66%, and for girls 22%. The figures for detention centres and borstals are no more cheering – 61% and 68% respectively for boys".[7]

Tutt concludes his book by recommending that approved schools in their present form be virtually abandoned. His alternative is the creation of small "corner shop" day-care centres offering education and training to young offenders and advice to their parents, while acting as a local facility for youth and adults (including night-stay accommodation). What Tutt describes is very similar to stage 9 on our continuum.

Residential care has four major disadvantages. These are, firstly, that the child is treated in an environment well away from the one which gave rise to his problems and to which he is returned, difficulties existing in his family and community remaining the same. Secondly, valuable supportive relationships developed with residential social workers during treatment are abruptly discontinued on discharge. Thirdly, there are relatively few opportunities for parental involvement and participation in the treatment of the child. Finally, as we have repeatedly stressed, the cost is prohibitive.

Highly intensive intermediate treatment, such as that described at stages 7 and 9 of the illustrative continuum in the previous chapter, might provide an alternative to full-time residential care. It is precisely these stages that approximate most closely to the provision of residential care, involving highly intensive supervision by full-time workers. (stage 8, short-term care, offering somewhat different forms of treatment would serve a slightly different purpose). And as we have already emphasised, to discharge children from residential care would release the resources necessary for setting up this segment of the continuum. It will be worthwhile investigating the structure of stages 7 and 9 in greater detail.

Stage 7

Refers to a pattern of treatment involving work with small groups on the basis of three nights per week and three weekends out of four. Children attending such a group would also be able to make us of night-stay facilities in crisis situations. They would also be able to make use of educational and occupational facilities in the communities in which they resided and in which their groups would be based.

The children selected for this type of intensive supervision would be those capable of using local education and trade-training facilities during the day. We would suggest that these facilities could best be provided in local colleges of further education, rather than in secondary schools. The atmosphere in these colleges is much more liberal and adult, and the trend is to encourage students to accept responsibility for their own learning. Small-group, or individual, tutorials are preferable to class-room learning for those who have had learning problems in schools. Certainly, individual educational needs could be better catered for in this type of setting.

Such a group could be of mixed sex, with a membership of no more than ten children, all of similar age. A programme of this kind might require specialist social work staff, who would also be the supervising officers, engaging in the necessary casework with families, and liaising closely with the schools, colleges and work situations of the children concerned. Overall child-staff ratio would be no greater than 3:1. Items in the programme would include all those referred to in the model scheme (Chapter 6), with special emphasis on the therapeutic element. A parallel parents' group, meeting one night a week, would ensure that feelings and situations of the family are constantly taken into account. The treatment group would have use of specific premises in the evening (which could well be the day-care centre of stage 9) and residential facilities for weekends and block weeks (which might correspond to the short-stay facility of stage 8). The cost of three or four full-time specialist intermediate treatment social workers would be about £10,000 per annum, while capital items, such as equipment and a mini-bus, would amount to £4,000. The group could also make use of local and national sporting/leisure facilities, and volunteer activity leaders could be involved. The principle of reorganisation and deployment of resources corresponds, of course, to that embodied in the description of the middle-range groups earlier in this chapter.

Stage 9

Represents day-care. Group size would be up to fifteen, comprising both sexes. The facility would consist of a large terrace house or council house, with night-stay accommodation in crisis situations (which could also be offered to groups at stage 7). The centre would be staffed by two teachers and two social workers, providing a programme of remedial education and trade-training, similar to that currently provided in community schools. Evening activities would take place under the direction of staff and volunteers. The social workers would do the family casework, and run a parellel parents' group similar to that involved at stage 7. Running costs: staff salaries would again amount to about £10,000 p.a. and capital costs would include: building and modifications, £30,000; mini-bus and equipment, £5,000.

Since both stages offer facilities to each other, the setting up of one facilitates the setting up of the other. This can be generalised, of course, for the entire continuum. Creating the continuum in the community will, of course, require a great deal of effort and imagination. It is not something that can be done without careful thought and planning, particularly with regard to the location of the day-care centre, appropriate "team" staffing, and selection of children for discharge from residential care where this is possible. Many adolescents, of course, may need to spend lengthy periods away from their families, and require hostel-type accommodation. The initial £45,000 required for stage 9 day care easily pays for itself, in view of the fact that two thirds of it is capital expenditure, and that the cost of maintaining fifteen children in residential care for only one year would be as much or greater. Moreover, the facility, once brought into being, would be a facility not only for stage 9 groups, but for other groups in the continuum.

Conclusion

It is not without significance that the recent Advisory Council on the Penal System has recommended a similar system of intensive supervision for young offenders aged 17-21.[8] The Council's proposals include a recommendation for a "supervision and control Order" for the community care of young men who might otherwise be committed to borstals, senior detention centres or prisons. The report dwells at some length on the apparent negative effects of custodial sentences and says:

> "The corollary to the growing awareness of the difficulties inherent in preparing young adults in custody to deal with the problems which will face them on release is that new ways must be found of controlling as many young offenders as possible without committing them to custody, and of bringing constructive influences to bear upon them while they continue to live and work in the community. Probation was, of course, the first step in this direction. Further steps now need to be taken . . . This can be achieved only by a deliberate switch of resources into a new system of control in the community".[9]

The recommendation here is for a *switch* of resources. As Terry Bamford has commented in *Social Work Today:*

> "It is idle to talk of more intensive supervision and of extending supervision to an increased number of young adult offenders without a massive reemployment of resources. The report leans heavily on the experience of California, but it is important to recall that California has made a switch of resources into probation by means of the "probation subsidy". The cost of building new custodial facilities will be enormous. It would be more sensible to allocate these resources to the probation service to enable it to adequately meet the new responsibilities".[10]

It is to be hoped that the Probation Service will take note of the experience of social services with regard to intermediate treatment, and that whatever facilities are offered for the supervision and control of young adult offenders, they will not be as inappropriate as those offered by the Regional Planning Committees with regard to adolescent offenders. Perhaps it would be advisable for the Probation Service to begin planning a continuum of care for clients currently in custody, so that a systematic treatment framework can be worked out in advance.

Of course, intermediate treatment as a social work method has applications right across the social work board. Many local authorities have day-centres the for elderly who, like the physically handicapped receive a number of services within the community which are specifically designed to support them and prevent the need for residential care. The "half-way" hostel concept for the mentally ill and handicapped is yet another "intermediate" provision, but the high re-admission rates of mental hospitals demonstrates the failure to implement community care policies. While the 1959 Mental Health Act proved the way for community based psychiatric social workers and the use of psychiatric day-centres, all too frequently, patients are shuttled between their families and hospital with little or no intermediate care. One gets the impression overall – highlighted now by the 1969 C.Y.P.A. – that no systematic planning has taken place which provides for varying intensities of "community care" – a broad concept which, like "intermediate treatment" can come to mean anything, or nothing. There is an urgent need for the creation of meaningful stages on a systematically thought out continuum of care for all those who, for the lack of such provision, ultimately end up in community homes, prisons, homes for the elderly and mental hospitals. Let us begin this process by taking greater care in our planning for children.

APPENDIX A

The Intermediate Treatment Development Group

1. The Albany Scheme, Lewisham.
   Based on reports by John Pitts, formerly Intermediate Treatment Organiser for Lewisham Social Services Department, now at North London Polytechnic, and his article in *Youth Social Work,* Vol. 1 No. 2.
2. Eastern Ravens Trust, Stockton-on-Tees.
   Contributed by Ian Waldram.
3. Haylands Junior Club, Bedford.
   Contributed by Keith Hiscock, of Bedfordshire Social Services Department.
4. Higher Clarence, Teesside.
   Based on a report by John Baldwin, now at Trent Polytechnic, Nottigham.
5. Islington Family Service Unit Intermediate Treatment Centre.
   Based on reports by the Centre staff, published the Islington Family Service Unit.
6. Northorpe Hall, Mirfield, Yorkshire.
   Based on the article in *Youth Service,* Vol.12 No.6 by Peter Hopkins, Director of Northorpe Hall.
7. Nottinghamshire Social Services Department.
   Based on material supplied by David Thorpe, formerly Development Officer for the department, and his article "Three Kinds of Intermediate Treatment" in *Social Work Today,* Vol.3 No.24.
8. Pontefract Handicraft Club and Activity Centre.
   Contributed by Robert Adams, Director of the Centre.
9. Youth Development Trust Project, Wythenshawe, Manchester.
   Contributed by Irene Naftalin, Project Leader.

Name, Location Area Code	Responsible Person or Body	Sex & Age Range	Nos.	Youth Club Times available	Specialist Club Time factors	Local Treatment Group	Local & Residential Treatment Group		Short-Term Care Max. Period	Day Care Overnight Facilities	Staffing		Social Work	Conditions & Procedure for Admission	Financial Arrangements	Programme (coded)
							Local	Res			Staff-Ratio	Type of Staff				
Haylands Junior Club		Boys 10-14	25		Wednesday 5.00 - 6.30 annual camp						1:4	youth 1. social w. stdnts.	supervisor involvement	referred by SW agencies and other members		a/b/c/i
Eastern Ravens		Boys & Girls 11-13	x8			26 weekly meetings weekend activities					1:4	youth w. vols.	after-care home visiting community	invitation after consultation		a/b/e/g
Youth Development Trust		Boys & Girls 11-16	7x10				weekly for 6 months	camps			1:3	gp wrker spvsr. CSW	supervisor parents group	supervisor participation 2 caseloads		a/b/e/g
Northorpe Hall		Boys 11-15	4x10					10 week-ends plus			1:3	group wrkrs	mid-week family casework	referred by SW agencies		a/b/c/e/g
Islington F.S.U. Intermediate Treatment Centre		Boys & Girls 12-15	15							for school non-attenders Mon-Thurs. 9.30 - 3.30	1:3	tchrs soc. wrkr. CSVs	community involvement	referred by school staff meet child & family		a/d/g/i

APPENDIX B

NOTES

Chapter 1

[1] Home Office, *Children in Trouble;* H.M.S.O., 1968.
[2] Op. cit., paragraph 2.
[3] *Children in Trouble,* paragraph 26.
[4] D.H.S.S., *Intermediate Treatment: a guide for the Regional Planning of new forms of treatment for children in trouble* (abbreviated as *Guide* in the text).
[5] Op. cit., Appendix C, paragraph 1.
[6] *Guide,* paragraph 15.
[7] National Youth Bureau Youth Social Work Unit: "Two Models of Intermediate Treatment", *Youth Social Work,* Vol.1 No.1.
[8] See, for example, Terry Powley's article, "Community-based Intermediate Treatment Services", *Youth Social Work,* Vol.1 No.3.
[9] Op. cit., paragraph 6.
[10] See Norman Tutt's discussion in *Care or Custody,* (Dartman, Longman & Todd, 1974) for example, p. 46-7.
[11] D.H.S.S., *Intermediate Treatment Project,* Chapter 1, paragraph 2.
[12] Tutt, op. cit., p. 209-10.
[13] See Tutt, op.cit., p. 49.
[14] D.H.S.S., *Intermediate Treatment Project,* Chapter 1, paragraph 2.

Chapter 2

[1] See, for example, *Survey of Full-Time Youth and Community Workers in the Education Service in England,* a report from the National Association of Youth Service Officers, October 1973.
[2] *Guide,* Chapter 2.
[3] *Children in Trouble,* Appendix C.
[4] *Guide,* Chapter 2, Paragraph 15.
[5] Four authorities in Yorkshire (Wakefield, Hull, Huddersfield and Bradford) had three requirements between them in the 6 month period beginning July 3rd 1973, when the regional scheme for Yorkshire came into effect. In the case of Bradford, 44 supervision orders made in favour of social services resulted in only one intermediate treatment requirement. See Richard Spencer's article "Slow Take-up" *Youth Social Work,* Vol.1 No.3.
[6] Spencer, op.cit.
[7] See Margaret Bone and Elizabeth Ross, *The Youth Service and Similar Provision for Young People* (H.M.S.O., 1972), especially Chapters 2 and 3.

[8]A literature sparked off by Mary Morse's *The Unattached* (Penguin, 1965).

[9]Ken Exton, "A Scheme of Assessment" in *Youth Social Work,* Vol.1 No.3.

[10] Exton, op.cit., and David Thorpe, "Three Kinds of Intermediate Treatment", in *Social Work Today,* Vol.3 No.24.

Chapter 3

[1]D.H.S.S. Development Group, *Intermediate Treatment Project*, H.M.S.O. 1973.

[2]Martin Rowntree, "An Introduction to Intermediate Treatment", in *Probation* Vol.17 No.1.

Chapter 5

[1]*Social Enquiry Reports and the Probation Service* (Martin Davies and Andrea Knopf) – Home Office Research Studies No.18, 1973.

[2]See Exton, *Individualised Justice and Treatment* (unpublished dissertation, School of Social Work, University of Leicester), and Dr. R. Ryall, *Delinquency: The Problem for Treatment in Social Work Today,* May 16th, 1974.

[3]For example, Stan Cohen, *Folk Devils and Moral Panics* (London, 1972).

[4]*Working Papers in Cultural Studies 2* (Spring 1972), published by the Centre for Contemporary Cultural Studies, University of Birmingham – see Paul Willis's paper. Also studies such as *Double Zero,* by David Collyer (Fontana, 1973).

[5]For example, Ernest Marms (Ed.), *Drugs and Youth: The Challenge of Today* (Pergamon, 1973).

[6]David Thorpe, "Putting Theory into Practice at Ryehill", in *Social Work Today.*

[7]David Hargreaves, "The Delinquent Subculture and the School", in W.G. Carson and Paul Wiles (Eds.), *Crime and Delinquency in Britain* (Martin Robertson, 1971).

[8]Power, M.J., Benn, R.T. and Morris, J.N., "Neighbourhood, School and Juveniles before the courts", in *British Journal of Criminology,* Vol.12, No.2.

[9]Hargreaves, op.cit.

[10] See C.M. Phillipson, "Juvenile Delinquency and the School", in Carson and Wiles, op.cit.

[11] Phillipson, op.cit.

[12] Islington Family Service Unit, *Intermediate Treatment Centre 2nd Report 1972-73.*

[13] C. Bagley, "Juvenile Delinquency in Exeter", quoted in J.B. Mays (Ed.), *Juvenile Delinquency, the Family and the Social Group* (Longman, 1972).

[14] Bagley, op.cit.
[15] Martin Davies, *Probationers in their Social Environment* (H.M.S.O., 1969).
[16] N.Y.B. Youth Social Work Unit, *Youth Social Work,* Vol.1 No.1.
[17] See, for example, Engels, "Crime and the Condition of the Working Class", reprinted in Carson and Wiles, op.cit.
[18] Sir Cyril Burt, *The Young Delinquent* (University of London, 1925).
[19] H.S. Becker, *Outsiders* (New York, 1963).
[20] See Hansard, Vol. 872, No.30: Written Answers (30 April, 1974). The exact figures (percentages of persons, aged between 10 and 17, cautioned of those found guilty or cautioned) are: Teesside – 11.8% and Devon and Cornwall – 64.8%.
[21] The expression is Alvin W. Gouldner's.

Chapter 6

[1] *Children in Trouble,* paragraph 25.
[2] The expression is used by Peter Righton as a title for his *Barnado Lecture* for 1973.

Chapter 7

[1] David Haxby, "Children in Trouble" in *Social Work Today,* Vol.3, No.22.
[2] Spencer, op.cit.
[3] Home Office Criminal Statistics, 1971 and 1972.
[4] N.Y.B. Youth Social Work Unit, op.cit.
[5] A. Greenwood-Wilson, "Punishment and Therapy" in *Community Schools Gazette,* January 1971.
[6] See Tutt, op.cit., especially p. 45-6.
[7] Tutt, op.cit., p. 46-7.
[8] The Advisory Council on the Penal System, *Young Adult Offenders,* 1974.
[9] *Young Adult Offenders,* Chapter 2, paragraph 21.
[10] Terry Bamford, "Young Adult Offenders", in *Social Work Today,* 27 June 1974.